Poetry Inspired by *A Midsummer Night's Dream*

A poetic anthology inspired by the plots and themes of William Shakespeare's comedy *A Midsummer Night's Dream*

Paul Gilliland

Editor-in-Chief

Southern Arizona Press

Southern Arizona Press

The mission of Southern Arizona Press is to promote the works of self-published and lesser-known unpublished authors and poets to the rest of the world through publishing themed and unthemed anthologies and assisting in the publication and promotion of their works.

It is our desire to make the voices of these aspiring poets and authors available to as wide an audience as possible with the belief that no writer of poetry or literature should ever have to pay to have their works published.

Hermia and Lysander 1870
John Simmons

Poetry Inspired by
A Midsummer Night's Dream

All rights reserved. Copyright © 2023 by Paul Gilliland and Southern Arizona Press. Except as permitted under the Copyright Act of 1976, no portion of this book may be reproduced or distributed in any form, or by any means without prior written consent of the individual authors or the publisher. Individual works Copyright © retained by the poetic author. Previously published works have been cited and each publication acknowledged to the best of our ability. If any citations have been missed, such errors will be corrected in subsequent reprints.

If you would like your work to be considered for future anthologies, please visit us at:
http://www.southernarizonapress.com/current-submissions/
for a full list of current open anthology submissions and submission guidelines.

Published by Southern Arizona Press
Sierra Vista, Arizona 85635
www.southernarizonapress.com

Follow us on Facebook at:
https://www.facebook.com/SouthernArizonaPress

Format, cover design, and edits by Paul Gilliland, Editor-in-Chief, Southern Arizona Press

Cover Art: *Hermia and Lysander (1870)* by John Simmons
Interior Art: As noted (Public Domain)

Poets photos Copyright © retained by submitting poets

ISBN: 9781960038258

Table of Contents

Lynn White   14

> *A New Day*
> *Dreaming*
> *Here Comes Summer*
> *Far Horizons, Distant Dreams*
> *Midsummer Madness*
> *Where is the Real World*

Teejay D. Panganiban   22

> *Magical Flight*
> *Money Can't Buy Happiness*
> *Shakespeare's Whimsical Play*
> *Memories of Love and Woes*
> *In the Stillness of the Night*

Michael H. San Miguel   28

> *Where the world is at peace and all is well*
> *The Enchanting Light*
> *A Day to Remember*
> *Rare Land*
> *From Romeo and Juliet's Secret Bond*

Laurice E. Tolentino   34

> *Enchanted Nuptials: A Midsummer Night's Dream Wedding*
> *Finding Hope Under the Moon Glow: A Midsummer Night's Dream*
> *Midsummer Dreams of a Little Boy*
> *Renewal in Midsummer Dreams of a Single Mother*
> *The Lady of Fairyland: Finding Love Under the Moon's Glow*

Kevin Ahern   42

Achoo
August Meditation
Daisy Leis
Homework
June

Avegail T. Paez   48

The Wedding Day
A Summer Vacation
Memories of Summer
The Fairy Land
Embracing the Summer

Nora V. Marasigan   54

A Toast to Love
The Woodland
The Realm of Fairy Land
Moonlit Shadows of Secret Love

Rp Verlaine   60

Atlantic City Moon
The Flower Moon's Eclipse
A Friend's Wedding
Storms and Leaves

Laura Helona Moverin   66

The Faery Kind
Dancers' Dream
Romantic Comedy
Litha

Pat Severin   72

> *Magic*
> *Solstice Triumph*
> *The Fairy's Spell*
> *My Dream*

Dennis Mitra Castillo   80

> *Enchanted Woodlands*
> *Lunar Mysticism*
> *Love and Magic*

Jerri Hardesty   84

> *Night Music*
> *Moonshine*
> *Summer Song*

Leanne Webber   88

> *A Litha Blessing*
> *My Mid-Summer Night's Dream*
> *Free?*

Diane Sahms   94

> *Cock-a-Hoop Night*

Binod Dawadi   96

> *A Midsummer Night's Dream*

Dibyasree Nandy   98

> *The White Night and the Black Sun*

Richard Oyama   102

> *Bottom's Bottom Dollar*
> *16/12/2022*

Ann Iverson   106

> *Moon Shadow*
> *Early Morning, Crescent Moon*

Andrew McDowell   110

> *Nighttime Crickets*

Rhiannon Owens   112

> *Midsummer Night*

Genalyn Panganiban-Lualhti   114

> *A Midsummer Night's Celebration*
> *Enchantment Under the Moonlight*

Ken Gosse   118

> *Perchance to Dream*

Loralyn Sandoval De Luna   120

> *Struggles of a Bewitched Human*

Gavin Prinsloo   122

> *Midsummer Morning*
> *Midsummer's Eve*

Kay Lesley Reeves   126

> *Ariel's Plea*

Joseph A. Farina   128

> *long night moon*
> *summer solstice*

Ken Allan Dronsfield   132

> *Songs of the Garden Chime*
> *Soft Silky Breeze*

Matt McGee   136

> *A Midsummer's Nightcap*

Erin Jamieson   142

> *A June Retelling*

Irma Kurti   144

> *The Immense Summer Sky*

Janet Ruth   146

> *The Door to Night is Ajar*
> *A Midsummer Day's Dream*

Joan McNerney   150

> *7 Summer Notes*
> *Summer Solstice*

Karen A. VandenBos   154

> *Night of the Long Sun*

Barbara Boothe Loyd   156

> *A Midsummer Night's Mix-up*

Marieta Maglas   158

> *Pantoum for Summer*

Gitanjli Mridul   160

> *A Midsummer Night*

Molly Howes   164

> *Summer Magic*

Lucia Lemieux   166

> *An Early Spring Morning's Dream*
> *Fae Folk in California*

Mary Ann Cabuyao Abril   170

> *Gift of Litha*
> *Your Hue*

Mark A. Fisher   174

> *Nick Bottom*
> *Puck Laughs*

Stephanie DuPont   177

> *A Dance Among the Chanterelles*

Regina Chriscel Santos Delute   180

> *The Dance of Love*

Paul Gilliland   182

>   *Fireflies and Fairies*
>   *Fairies at Night*
>   *The Shooting Star of Romance*
>   *An Evening in Early June*
>   *Summer Nights*
>   *Summer Solstice Sun*

**Previous anthologies from
   Southern Arizona Press   190**

**Upcoming anthologies from
   Southern Arizona Press   192**

**New independent releases from
   Southern Arizona Press   194**

Published works by our featured contributors   198

**Lynn White** lives in north Wales. Her work is influenced by issues of social justice and events, places, and people she has known or imagined. She is especially interested in exploring the boundaries of dream, fantasy, and reality. She was shortlisted in the Theatre Cloud 'War Poetry for Today' competition and has been nominated for a Pushcart Prize, Best of the Net, and a Rhysling Award. Her poetry has appeared in many publications including: *Apogee*, *Firewords*, *Capsule Stories*, *Gyroscope Review*, and *So It Goes*.

Find Lynn at:

https://lynnwhitepoetry.blogspot.com
https://www.facebook.com/Lynn-White-Poetry-1603675983213077/

Poetry Inspired by "A Midsummer Night's Dream"

A New Day

The loss of light comes earlier,
that's when the day ends
and the night begins.
And then,
strangely
a new day begins
at midnight
in the middle of the night
when darkness is at its
blackest,
its most intense
and only the night owls
are out and about
heaving their midnight sighs
for the new day to come
and the one they've lost.

First published in *Flights of the Dragonfly Issue 2*, September 2021.

Dreaming

'To sleep perchance to dream'.
That's what he said.
Sounds so gentle,
but there's a rub,
a rough edge to this sleepy escape
that would see me float away
sending me spinning,
out of control
tumbling,
raging,
spiralling,
crashing
to an indeterminate end.

So perhaps it's daytime dreaming
that has the edge
to smoothly move me
from one place to another.
In wakeful dreams
I can determine the beginning,
at least,
and invite the participants.
Sometimes
they may act out an old story
with a predictable end.
Sometimes
I can write a new story
and then

bring it to life.

First published in *Flights of the Dragonfly* Issue 2, September 2021.

Poetry Inspired by "A Midsummer Night's Dream"

Here Comes Summer

Here comes summer.
Long days of bright sunshine
and shiny warm evenings
stretching into starry nights.
We have waited a long time for the thaw,
for the ice to melt
away.
Sometimes the clouds gather briefly,
the dark ones,
not the fluffy whites.
Sometimes there's a shower of rain,
perhaps refreshing,
perhaps thundery
when the clouds let fall their tears.
But for now there's warmth and heat
and pleasure
with warm moist days to follow
when the sweet leaves begin to fall.
And a winter of blue skies
belying the cold,
so we can almost believe that summer is still
with us
and we are not lost as the freezing fog
descends
to envelop us
again.

First published in *Blognostics*, June 2019.

Far Horizons, Distant Dreams

Once the light shone so brightly
that time and distance stretched for ever,
the horizon at infinity strung with the pearls
of distant dreams.
And in between
a hinterland
of possibilities
just waiting to be grasped.
But then, as the light dimmed,
time and distance collapsed inwards
dragging the horizon closer
a hinterland
of rubble
in between,
the spent remains
of possibilities
uncompleted
or untried.
Only the dreams stretched further
beyond the horizon now
in the fading light.
Soon I'll reach them
and perhaps discover myself
as part of someone else's dream.

First published in *Lion And Lilac*, August 2021.

Poetry Inspired by "A Midsummer Night's Dream"

Midsummer Madness

I saw a rabbit in the clouds
it was eating something,
but what was it?
Didn't look like a carrot,
more like an ice cream cone,
well it was a hot day.
Perhaps it was no rabbit
but a hare with a touch of
midsummer madness.
Later it re arranged itself
and became a cat,
quite definitely cat,
a Cheshire Cat
no doubt about it
hoping to join Hare and Alice
at the tea party.
And who knows,
if the White Rabbit is on time
maybe he'll bring ice cream for all.
Anything can happen
on a midsummer
afternoon.

First published in *Free Verse Revolution, Obscure Illusions,* March 27 2021.

Where is the Real World

There was a broken circle in my field of wheat this morning.
Can't explain it.
Walked through the wheat scratching my head with a stalk.
Can't explain.
There are shapes in the circle, shapes which look like
the shapes and spaces of this world. Lands and seas.
Can't explain them.

Fell asleep in the scratchy stalks of my field in the sunshine.
Can't say why.
Awoke in England, I think, lying there, floating above it,
I think.
Lying here, drifting away, like a balloon out of control,
but avoiding the sun and the stars and the other worlds.
I think.

Or am I lying below, in my field with my heels on the ground?
Difficult to know.
Hard to discern this place and know my place in it.
Can't explain
why I'm floating here, unsure if I'm drifting above or below.
I might fall. I might fall up or down. I don't know which.
Can't explain my confusion.

But, I'll know when I stop spinning round, seeing the stars
in the sunshine.
But how will I get down if I'm already below, my heels grounded
in reality,
in England, in my field of wheat, scratching my head, looking,
up at the shapes in the space of the sky drifting above me.
Can't explain.

First published by Pilcrow and Dagger, *Midsummer Night's Dream Issue*, June, 2015.

Oberon and Titania – Act II, Scene III
by Charles Mottram (1817-1876)

 **Dr. Teejay D.Panganiban** is an instructor for the undergraduate teacher education programs teaching major and professional courses at Batangas State University, The National Engineering University, JPLPC-Malvar. At present, he handles various designations such as the Program Chairperson for the Bachelor in Physical Education, Head of the Culture and Arts, Adviser of Melophiles Band, Adviser of Human Kinetics Society, and Head Coach for Sepaktakraw Team of the university.

His passion in sports, music, and arts was translated into research articles where he has published his works in *Scopus Indexed Journals*, CHED accredited journal and international peer-reviewed journal with sterling reputation. Also, his research papers were presented in national and international research fora and served as adviser and panel member for student research in the college.

He believes in the value of arming physical education students with practical, lifelong, and health skills, which cross over subject matter in order to develop a character for a positive personal, family, and community life.

Poetry Inspired by "A Midsummer Night's Dream"

Magical Flight

In fair Athens town, where dreams are born,
A tale of love and magic was sworn.
The fairies dance in the moonlit night,
As lovers chase their hearts' delight.

Oberon and Titania, the king and queen,
Rule over the woods, their magic seen.
But when they feud, the world goes awry,
And humans caught in the middle, sigh.

Hermia and Lysander, Helena and Demetrius,
Their tangled love, a source of fuss.
Puck, the mischievous sprite, causes confusion,
As the lovers' emotions reach their conclusion.

But in the end, all is made right,
Love conquers all, in the fairy's sight.
The play within the play, a merry delight,
A Midsummer Night's Dream, a magical flight.

Money Can't Buy Happiness

On your wedding day, remember this truth,
Money can't buy happiness, it's not proof,
Of the love you share, or the bond you hold,
No amount of wealth can replace pure gold.

For what you have is something unique,
A love that's real, and one that's complete,
It's not based on riches or material things,
But on the joy that true love brings.

It's the way you look into each other's eyes,
And the way you hold each other tight,
It's the laughter and the tears you share,
And the way you show each other you care.

So on this special day, don't let money rule,
But let your love be the shining jewel,
That brings you happiness and joy each day,
And keeps your love growing in every way.

For in the end, it's not the money or the fame,
But the love you share that will remain,
So cherish it always, and hold it tight,
And your love will shine forever bright.

Poetry Inspired by "A Midsummer Night's Dream"

Shakespeare's Whimsical Play

In the enchanted woods, where fairies play,
A world of wonder and magic holds sway.
Here, love is but a fleeting dream,
As mischief reigns supreme.

Titania, queen of the fairy realm,
Falls under the spell of Oberon's helm.
Puck, the mischievous sprite,
Brings chaos with all his might.

Lysander and Demetrius, both in love with fair Hermia,
Elope into the woods, where they meet with the faerie,
Who casts a spell that makes them both love Helena,
And chaos ensues, as their affections warp and bend.

Meanwhile, the mechanicals prepare a play,
To perform before the Duke and his bride-to-be one day.
But Oberon, with mischief on his mind,
Sends Puck to switch Bottom's head, a jest unkind.

Amidst the chaos and the laughter,
The lovers' true hearts are what really matter.
As they wake from their enchanted dreams,
Love triumphs, as it always seems.

And so, in Shakespeare's whimsical play,
We see love and magic in equal sway.
A Midsummer Night's Dream, a tale so bright,
That still enchants us to this very night.

Memories of Love and Woes

In the heart of a forest deep and green,
Where magic and mischief reign supreme,
A Midsummer Night's Dream unfolds,
As love and laughter take hold.

Titania, queen of the faerie folk,
Lies slumbering beneath an enchanted cloak,
While Puck, mischievous sprite of the wood,
Causes chaos as only he could.

Lovers lost in a tangle of desire,
Fickle as flames, their hearts set afire,
As the mischievous Puck plays his game,
Mistaken identities drive them insane.

But love prevails in the end,
As they all come to comprehend,
That true love is not just skin deep,
And sometimes, it's better to take a leap.

And so, as the moon rises high,
And the stars twinkle in the sky,
A Midsummer Night's Dream comes to a close,
Leaving us with memories of love and woes.

Poetry Inspired by "A Midsummer Night's Dream"

In the Stillness of the Night

As the sun sets and the day is done,
The light of the moon has just begun.
Casting its silver glow upon the land,
Guiding the nocturnal creatures with a steady hand.

In the stillness of the night,
The moon's radiance shines so bright,
Illuminating the path we tread,
As we journey towards our bed.

Beneath its watchful eye,
The world takes on a different guise,
As shadows dance and flicker,
And the night air becomes much thicker.

Oh, light of the moon, so fair and bright,
Guiding us through the darkness of the night,
A constant companion in our time of need,
A beacon of hope and a symbol of peace indeed.

So let us embrace the light of the moon,
And revel in its serene and calming tune,
As we find solace in its gentle glow,
And let our worries and troubles go.

#

Michael H. San Miguel is an instructor for the undergraduate teacher education programs at Batangas State University TNEU JPLPC-Malvar. He is also a research-based faculty member who is trained in quantitative, qualitative, and mixed methodologies of research in the same university. He has published research articles on Physical Education and Sports pedagogy and educational management in CHED accredited journal and international peer-reviewed journal with sterling reputation. Currently, he is working as the Head for office of Sports Development Program, and Head Coach for the Athletics team of the Batangas State University system.

Where the world is at peace and all is well

In the woodland, where nature's at play,
The trees whisper secrets to those who stay.
A place of mystery, wild and free,
Where the world is as it's meant to be.

With rustling leaves and the rustling sound,
The woodland invites all to come around,
And venture in with curious eyes,
To discover what nature hides.

In the shadows of the trees so tall,
Creatures scurry and birds do call,
The woodland's secrets are kept so well,
A place where magic and mystery dwell.

The rustling leaves and the babbling brook,
A soothing sound that you cannot overlook,
As you wander down the winding path,
It's hard to resist nature's soothing bath.

The woodland's beauty is hard to describe,
A place where nature can truly thrive,
Where the world is at peace and all is well,
In the woodland where nature doth dwell.

The Enchanting Light

Under the light of the moon,
Shakespeare's words begin to swoon,
As the night grows dark and still,
His tales come to life with skill.

Romeo and Juliet's tragic fate,
Or Hamlet's mind in a troubled state,
The magic of the bard's pen,
Brings forth emotions time and again.

In the glow of the lunar beams,
His characters dance in our dreams,
Their stories told so long ago,
Yet their impact we still know.

Under the light of the moon,
Shakespeare's legacy continues to bloom,
As we bask in his literary prowess,
And marvel at his timeless progress.

So let us raise a glass in honor,
Of the poet who was a master planner,
Whose works remain forever bright,
Under the moon's enchanting light.

Poetry Inspired by "A Midsummer Night's Dream"

A Day to Remember

A wedding is a day to remember
A time when two hearts unite
In the presence of friends and family
To celebrate their love so bright

Today we gather to witness
The joining of two souls
Bound together by commitment
And love that forever grows

The bride in all her beauty
With a smile that lights up the room
The groom, handsome and dashing
As they stand together, love blooms

The rings exchanged as a symbol
Of the love they share today
A promise to be faithful
In every possible way

As they embark on their journey
Together as husband and wife
May their love continue to flourish
And their hearts remain full of life

Let us raise a glass in honor
Of this beautiful union today
May their love be strong and steadfast
Forever and always, we pray.

Rare Land

In the realm of Fairyland,
Where mischief and magic go hand in hand,
A world of sprites and faeries reside,
With secrets and wonders that cannot be denied.

The Puck and Oberon, the fairy king,
Rule the land where dreams take wing,
And Titania, the queen, with grace and might,
Enchants all who enter her sight.

The fairies dance in the moonlight glow,
And their laughter echoes as they go,
Their wings aflutter, their steps so light,
As they play and frolic throughout the night.

But beware, for mischief lies in store,
For fairies can be tricksy and more,
And those who dare to wander too far,
May find themselves caught in a fairy jar.

So heed the warnings and take care,
In the realm of Fairyland, so rare,
For magic and wonder await within,
But mischief and mayhem can easily begin.

Poetry Inspired by "A Midsummer Night's Dream"

From Romeo and Juliet's Secret Bond

In fair Verona, where we lay our scene,
The stage is set for love, the heart's queen,
As Shakespeare's weddings come to life,
And lovers bind in joyful strife.

The maidens decked in silken gowns,
The men in doublets of finest browns,
Their hearts ablaze with passion's fire,
Their vows made with unrelenting desire.

From Romeo and Juliet's secret bond,
To Titania and Oberon's fairy pond,
Love blooms in all its varied forms,
In Shakespeare's tales, a heart that warms.

But weddings in his plays are not all bright,
For some, they mark a tragic plight,
As Desdemona's union with Othello ends,
And the bride's father mourns and bends.

Yet still, the weddings in his works inspire,
To love, to cherish, to never tire,
To find a soul mate, a kindred heart,
And never let love's fire depart.

So let us celebrate the Bard's wit and art,
And the weddings that played a part,
In his timeless tales of love and grace,
That continue to inspire the human race.

**Laurice E. Tolentino** is an Instructor at Batangas State University TNEU JPLPC- Malvar, Philippines where she instructs Professional and General Education courses for programs in College of Teacher Education as well as Major subjects for programs in International Hospitality Management. For the past two years, she has served as the College of Teacher Education's research coordinator and most recently in-charge as Food Services at the same university. In addition, she served as the Faculty Advisor for the Junior Hotelier and Restaurateur Association's (JHRA) from (2008-2010, 2016-2018 & 2020-2022). From 2016 to 2020, she worked as an OJT Coordinator for IHM Students.

Within her personal life, she has a strong interest in advancement and self-development. She is constantly looking for fresh challenges and opportunities to acquire new skills which highlight her values for learning new things and for improving oneself.

Poetry Inspired by "A Midsummer Night's Dream"

Enchanted Nuptials: A Midsummer Night's Dream Wedding

In my dream, a Midsummer's night,
Beneath the stars, so warm and bright,
I walk down the aisle with grace,
A smile of joy upon my face.

The flowers in my hair so fair,
Matched the bouquet that I bear,
A vision in my flowing gown,
In which I feel like a queen crowned.

The fairy lights around us twirl,
As we dance under the enchanted world,
The magic of Midsummer's night,
Filling the air with sheer delight.

The tables in the gardens spread,
With flowers and candles, a sight to behold,
As we feast on the finest fare,
In the company of those who care.

The music fills the air with love,
As we share the first dance under the stars above,
And as the night draws to a close,
We'll never forget this dream that flows.

For in this Midsummer's night dream,
Our love and happiness forever gleam,
And though the dream may fade away,
Our love will forever stay.

Finding Hope Under the Moon's Glow: A Midsummer Night's Dream

Under the light of the moon,
A girl sits all alone,
Her heart heavy with gloom,
Her spirit all but flown.

She weeps and sighs in pain,
Lost in thoughts and memories,
Of love that was in vain,
And dreams that were not meant to be.

But in the midst of her despair,
The fairies of Midsummer's night,
Appear before her without a care,
And fill her heart with delight.

They dance and sing around her,
And sprinkle fairy dust in the air,
And the girl begins to wonder,
If there's still magic left to spare.

The girl takes a deep breath,
And lets herself be swept away,
By the fairies' enchanting breath,
And the magic of this night's sway.

Under the light of the moon so bright,
The girl begins to see,
That there is still hope in sight,
And her heart can once again be free.

Poetry Inspired by "A Midsummer Night's Dream"

For in the realm of fairyland,
Anything is possible and more,
And under the light of the moon's hand,
Sadness can become joy, forevermore.

So the girl dances and sings,
With the fairies of the night,
And in her heart, a new hope rings,
Under the moon's enchanting light.

Midsummer Dreams of a Little Boy

In the midst of summer's eve,
A little boy did dream,
Of fairies dancing in the trees,
And magic streams that gleamed.

He closed his eyes and saw it all,
A world so wondrous and bright,
Where woodland creatures came to call,
And the stars shone all through the night.

The little boy laughed and danced,
As the fairies twirled around,
Their wings a blur in the moonlit glade,
Their laughter a sweet, melodic sound.

He chased the fireflies through the grass,
And caught them in his hand,
As the world around him seemed to pass,
In a dream that was grand.

And when the night did finally end,
And the sun began to rise,
The little boy knew he'd found a friend,
In the magic of the midsummer skies.

For though the dream had come and gone,
The memories would always stay,
A little boy's midsummer night's dream,
A magical tale to tell one day

Poetry Inspired by "A Midsummer Night's Dream"

Renewal in Midsummer Dreams of a Single Mother

In the midst of summer's heat,
A single mother fell asleep,
And in her dreams, a world complete,
A place where hope and love did seep.

She saw herself in a meadow fair,
Surrounded by a glowing light,
A warm breeze blowing through her hair,
As the stars lit up the night.

In this place, she felt at ease,
Her worries and fears all gone,
She danced and laughed with such great ease,
As she moved to nature's song.

The fairies danced around her feet,
As she twirled in joyful glee,
And in her heart, she felt so sweet,
A love that set her spirit free.

In this dream, she found her strength,
Her courage and her light,
And as the night began to lengthen,
She knew she'd win the fight.

For though the world was tough and cruel,
Her dreams gave her a respite,
A single mother's midsummer night's dream,
A place where everything felt right.

So when she woke, she felt renewed,
With hope and love within her heart,
A single mother, strong and true,
Ready for a brand new start

The Lady of Fairyland: Finding Love Under the Moon's Glow

In the realm of fairyland,
Amidst the magic and the grand,
There lived a lady fair,
With beauty beyond compare.

Her hair was like the sun's gold,
Her eyes like the stars of old,
Her smile could light up the night,
And make everything feel all right.

She danced with grace and ease,
As if she were one with the breeze,
And her voice was sweet and clear,
Like the song of the lark so dear.

For though she lived in fairyland,
Where dreams and magic were at hand,
Her heart longed for something more,
Something that she'd not felt before.

And so she wandered through the land,
Hoping to find what she could not understand,
Until one day, under the moon's glow,
She met a man who made her heart flow.

For in his eyes, she saw the light,
That had been missing from her sight,
And in his touch, she felt the love,
That she'd been searching for above.

Poetry Inspired by "A Midsummer Night's Dream"

And so in the realm of fairyland,
The lady found her heart's demand,
And with the man, she lived a life,
Filled with love, laughter, and light.

For in the realm of fairyland,
Anything is possible and grand,
And under the moon's enchanting sway,
Love can find a new, eternal way.

 **Kevin Ahern** is a Professor Emeritus of biochemistry from Oregon State University who is enjoying the spare time he has gained in retirement to write verses, limericks, and other creative items.

Poetry Inspired by "A Midsummer Night's Dream"

Achoo

This year on our summer vacation
One place caused us great aggravation
The dry summer breezes
Caused too many sneezes
When we stopped at our first dusty nation

August Meditation

Oh summer, how the time we savored
Such great fun with you
A brief release for good behavior
But ending, now it's true

Motor homers packed all day
Crammed their vans, then drove away
These people really have odd zen
Getting away from it all
Means taking it with them

Poetry Inspired by "A Midsummer Night's Dream"

Daisy Leis

"Orchids don't bloom well in July
That time in Hawaii's a bummer
So when substitutions are made
They're known as the Daisy Leis of Summer"

Homework

The gard'ning instructor's dictation
Gave students some real consternation
"No more dirty looks"
"Work hard on your books"
"And weed on your summer vacation"

Poetry Inspired by "A Midsummer Night's Dream"

June

The month of June's the longest one
At least in terms of light
The solstice brings a sun that steals
Hours away from night

And with the light, our spirits sing
A joyous summer song
We've got all our vacations planned
Let's hope it's not too long

Cuz pools and beaches beckon us
Our swimsuits so revealing
And if you overdo the sun
Your skin finds it a peeling

 **Avegail T. Paez** is a Professor of Mathematics and the Quality Assurance Head at Bulacan State University-Meneses Campus. She received her Master's degree in Master of Arts in Education Major in Mathematics at the Bulacan State University. Her recent publication is as one of the authors/translator of the book *Culture: No Longer Invisible in Language Learning but an Equal Status Strand. Teaching Languages through Intercultural Literature, Much More than Archipelago* (2018), *Tales from the Philippines*. A research project between the Bulacan State University and the University of Valencia, Spain. She is now currently on the phase 1 of the approved funded research from the university on the Structural Equation Model of the Impact of Teachers' Self-Efficacy on Students' Motivation and Achievement. Also, currently is on the process of completing a translation for publication of her creative works titled, *Guro* and *Padayon Guro*.

Poetry Inspired by "A Midsummer Night's Dream"

The Wedding Day

On this momentous day, two hearts were intertwined.
As they promise to love unconditionally,
Every word they speak is a sign of their affection.
on their wedding day, the bride and the groom.

The bride enters the church, glowing and fair.
Putting flowers in her hair while wearing a flowing robe,
Her heart is racing with unfathomable love.
As she approaches her waiting husband.

They both stood together in front of family and friends.
Their unwavering love is a lighthouse.
Vows are exchanged, transcending time as they are forever.
a blossoming affection that never sags.

They exchange rings as a sign of their love,
To uphold and surpass a promise made,
They work hand in glove to confront the future together.
In all, with love and joy.

The event starts with dancing and joy.
This magnificent night, they celebrate
A absolutely spectacular sight, with toasts and speeches
A wedding day filled with sunshine and love.

So let us rejoice in this wonderful event.
A wedding day filled with joy,
Without hesitation, a love promise
A friendship that endures beyond comprehension.

A Summer Vacation

Summer break is a time to explore.
To break free from the monotony of daily life,
To travel far or to stay close to home,
And travel the world on our own.

The countless hours of bright sunlight,
A promise of adventure and enjoyment,
The warmth that permeates our bones,
As we bask on the throne of nature.

The sandy beaches, with such tremendous waves,
The roar of the ocean, a lullaby
The seagulls flying through the sky,
Nature's sigh symphony.

The mountains, with their towering summits,
A world of wonder is at our disposal.
The treks and climbs that we direct,
A challenge that makes us feel so accomplished.

The vibrant cities, with their vivid sights,
A wonderland filled of brightness,
The nearby museums, parks, and stores,
A truly enjoyable journey.

So let us enjoy this time of year.
And all the delight it provides us,
Because in these open and pure moments,
We discover the essence of life's cheer.

Poetry Inspired by "A Midsummer Night's Dream"

Memories of Summer

In summer's heat and golden glow,
Memories of youth begin to flow,
Of lazy days without a care,
And precious moments we still share.

The sound of waves against the shore,
The sunsets that we would adore,
Long nights spent beneath the stars,
Making wishes from afar.

The scent of blooming flowers near,
The taste of ice cream we hold dear,
The warmth of sunshine on our skin,
These are the memories within.

The laughter of friends fills the air,
As we make memories without a care,
Summer days that we hold so dear,
Remain in our hearts throughout the year.

Though time may pass and summers fade,
These memories will never be betrayed,
For they are treasures we can keep,
In our hearts forever to reap.

The Fairy Land

Fairyland, where enchantment reigns supreme,
A universe of wonder with no boundaries,
Where fairies and unicorns frolic,
And in every manner, dreams come true.

The tall trees in the wooded glades
A mysterious world enthralled by sprites
The vibrant colors of the meadow's blossoms
A beautiful place in every way.

The fairies, who have iridescent wings,
Flutter and fly with such grace,
Their laughter reverberates in the morning dew.
And their magic is a gift that is both pure and new.

There is no such thing as time or aging in Fairyland.
A land of innocence, where love reigns supreme
In the emerald water, the mermaids swim.
And the fireflies are gleefully dancing.

The unicorns, with their magnificent horns,
Fairyland, graze in the fields,
Their surprise, their magic, is absolutely magnificient
Each thread is a sign of purity.

So follow me to Fairyland's joy.
Where enchantment flourishes and dreams soar,
And wonder and beauty are around.
In Fairyland, where everything is perfect.

Embrace the Summer

Summer's sun-kissed days,
Where there is light and freedom,
The golden light's warmth,
To me, it's a comforting balm.

The fragrance of budding flowers,
Every color and tint,
The lovely scent of freshly cut grass,
That fades into the distance.

The echoing sound of laughing
Children who are playing outside
They are splashing and swimming in the pool.
With unending joy and pride.

The flavors of fresh fruits and ice cream
A truly delicious treat,
As we appreciate each morsel of food,
In the midst of summer.

The cool breeze,
It rustles through the branches.
On sweltering days, it's a welcome relief.
A moment to unwind.

The memories we make,
In this season of heat and fun,
Are precious stones that we hold,
That gleams brilliantly in the sunlight.

So, let us enjoy the summer.
And all the joys it offers,
For in these moments of absolute ecstasy,
We can find the most basic things in life.

 **Dr. Nora V. Marasigan** is a Filipino associate professor in the undergraduate and graduate teacher education programs at Batangas State University JPLPC-Malvar. As an educator, she is primarily interested in conducting studies on mathematics and mathematics education which focus on topics essential to educational innovations. She has been invited as a resource speaker in seminars/webinars dealing with Mathematics teaching and learning, test construction and analyzing research data. She is a mathematics professor and has published research articles on mathematics, mathematics education and pedagogy in international peer-reviewed journal. She has also published creative works in a multidisciplinary academic publisher and won the Best Poetry and Best Short Story Awards in the Cape Comorin Writers' Festival 2020.

Poetry Inspired by "A Midsummer Night's Dream"

A Toast to Love

A wedding day, a blissful spot,
As two hearts come together tight,
But love can be a fitful thing,
And havoc can arrive on the scene.

In lovely Athens, a Duke got married,
But love triangles reared their head,
A naughty Puck caused much strife,
But love conquered all in the night.

With fairies in attendance there,
The wedding feast was full of cheer,
When daybreak came, everything was fit
Dazzling triumph of love in its wake

So let us toast to love's sweet might,
And pray that it will guide us right,
For when true love is really found,
The world is brighter, full of delight.

Southern Arizona Press

The Woodland

The woodland, full of life and light,
Where freedom sways both day and night,
A place where love and laughter grow,
And all our cares just cease to flow.

In Arden's forest, we find love,
As Rosalind, disguised, did act,
Her lover Orlando, captivated so,
Their passion bloomed, pure and true.

The forest also hides a snake,
As scheming Duke did plan and make,
But justice served and all was right,
And love did win, to our delight.

So let us wander, free and bold,
In woodland glades both young and old,
For love and laughter, all can find,
And leave our worries far behind

Poetry Inspired by "A Midsummer Night's Dream"

The Realm of Fairy Land

Amidst the woods, in fairy home,
Where nymphs and pixies roam,
The magic merged by Puck's own hand
Turns hearts of mortals to stone

But love, oh love, it conquers all,
And breaks the spell to them bestowed
As Lysander and Hermia's power
Is shattered by love's holler

The realm of fairy land, so bright,
Where nighttime is turned to daylight,
Enchantment reigns with all its might,
And wondrous visions come to light

So let us delight in this land,
Where dreams and love wrap around,
And where the magic Puck has planned,
Will make our hearts bring into line.

Moonlit Shadows of Secret Love

Under the light of the moon so bright,
Two lovers met in silence around,
Their love hindered by their clans,
Their ardor deep, their souls within

Their families' dispute, a fuming fire,
Threatens to quench out their desire,
But in each other's arms they find,
The comfort of a love so kind

Yet fate is vicious, and tragedy looms,
As their love is met with brutal dooms,
And under the light of the moon they part,
Their love forever engraved in heart.

Oh, dreadful love, so pure and true,
Under the moonlit shadows, we knew,
That love, though banned, can ignite,
The spark that makes our hearts take flight.

Poetry Inspired by "A Midsummer Night's Dream"

Titania sleeping in the moonlight protected by her fairies
John Simmons (1823-1876)

 **Rp Verlaine** lives in New York City. He has an MFA in creative writing from City College. He taught in New York Public schools for many years. His first volume of poetry - *Damaged by Dames & Drinking* was published in 2017 and another – *Femme Fatales Movie Starlets & Rockers* in 2018. A set of three e-books titled *Lies From The Autobiography vol 1-3* were published from 2018 to 2020. His latest book, *Imagined Indecencies*, was published in February of 2022. He was nominated for a Pushcart Prize in poetry in 2021 and 2022.

Poetry Inspired by "A Midsummer Night's Dream"

Atlantic City Moon
For Theresa

The shore's crisp cool air and the naked moon
casting light on sins that await judgment
while my head won't clear after too much gin.
Atlantic City where it's just me and the loons
laughing at fate we couldn't circumvent
that foiled us while somewhere the devil grinned.
Theresa its been years -yet I see you
dancing in a short dress my eyes still hold
as a truth dark nights since haven't let go.
Your smile a sarong around my soul
a hangman's jealousy might know up close.
Theresa dance under the skies tonight
to music in my heart missing your light.

The Flower Moon's Eclipse

That all too bright dear sentinel and sphere
with mocking eyes only the earth's eclipse
can shadow with veils of departing dark.
A curtain fit to hide that which was clear
to lovers passions blind with each new twist
till fortune leaves but wounds and gaping scars.
Discovery hides much: these perfumed nights
when lovers walk so close they seem entwined
content as sparrows circling in their midst.
Yet those unloved - walk in revealing light
with false and heavy step like awkward mimes
wanting dark of the flower moon's eclipse.
Welcoming its brief veil which shields the pain
obfuscating tears better than the rain.

Poetry Inspired by "A Midsummer Night's Dream"

A Friend's Wedding

The warmth, I welcome after winter's chill
captured in letters where large tears have dried.
From one I thought for good, even for ill
I'd marry come the shadows of July.
Rare was her beauty, yet her greatest gift
was her keen wit and a splendid style
in her dress and dance, 'twas almost as if
the gods looked down upon her just to smile.
I was envied by many close dear friends
save one who circled us with much intrigue.
Used lies and gossip to put a sad end
to lovers he both envied and deceived.
Worse, it seems she will keep that wedding day
with he, I called friend, who stole her away.

Storms And Leaves

After a bad breakup
the wide space
of loneliness and
the uncertain grip
of doubt does
us both in
and we are
together
anew
feeling the gentle
and unbroken peace
of two souls
in the
same calm
swaying hammock
the wind is
finally gentle with.

Daring to not
tip us over
yet…
until
the next storm
brewing
like
fallen leaves
slowly
gathering
ever circling
rapidly in warnings
that we shall
again, not heed.

Poetry Inspired by "A Midsummer Night's Dream"

Titania and Bottom c 1790
Henry Fuseli (1741-1825)

**Laura Helona Moverin** is a queer Brisbane based writer and poet. She works with teenagers as a librarian. A love of writing and words is a hazard of the profession. Laura came to Australia from Africa as a child as part of the exodus of the 80's. She has three disabilities that keep life interesting.

The Faery Kind

Curious fire globes,
Drift in a forest outside Athens
Among the oaks and aspens.
Spin higher, take fire.
The burning brand
Is passed from hand to hand,
Weaving in a circle towards completion
Echoing in symmetry the celestial dance,
To purify these heavy forms
Into lighter wind born creatures,
The Faery kind their pixie features
Masks of delight and glee
And solemnity when they glance at the moon,
Their goddess floating high
Wide and stately globe in the sky,
Her silver tresses descending
Like a future that is still pending,
They are waiting for the dawn
To swarm into the deep hollows.

Dancers' Dream

Good morning stars, sunshine light
Illuminate the stage in turn,
As the dancers intertwine and imitate
The tangled shapes of vegetation,
They leave soft traces behind
The sounds of sliding feet
Their gliding forms compete
Some are lifted high.
They glitter in clouds of taffeta.
They puff and heave like horses
Even the donkey.
Play your smiling tricks puck,
Role and kick your legs with laughter.
Prevent the lovers meeting,
Keep their touches fleeting,
As they spin and collide in mock fight
Grotesque but comic with it.

Poetry Inspired by "A Midsummer Night's Dream"

Romantic Comedy

Let me start by finding the joy.
I don't want to bring you anger or sorrow
Not mockery or malicious laughter,
Merely a chuckle at the irony of being human
Like the best of Shakespeare's plays.
Our confusions, our delusions
Tickle the fancy of the gods,
They think it odd
That we don't speak straight.
They watch us run and arrive to late,
Then find a flower seller in the rain
Yes I've been watching those films again.
There's something comic about love,
Helping us to laugh despite the pain
It does me good to smile,
Again and again and again.

Litha

This is the festival of Litha
Rejoice for we have come to the longest day of the year
The sun has ridden his chariot to the zenith
    and smiles brightly on us
He smiles on the earth and the Summer Queen blossoms
She brings forth fruit, flowers and grain
Sunflowers and corn rise with the rain
Be joyful now, let the children come running
Because as I speak the year is turning
The Holly king steps forward to battle with his brother
The Oak king must fall and surrender his crown
The Holly king's bright blood is on the robins breast
He howls like the wolf full of life and zest
Because he is victorious
Autumn and winter may come
Thus fulfilling the journey of all the seasons

Poetry Inspired by "A Midsummer Night's Dream"

Oberon, Titania, and Puck with Fairies Dancing c.1786
William Blake

**Pat Severin**, a retired teacher and member of SCBWI, has been writing poetry for many years. Her poems are regularly featured in the online magazines, *The Agape Review*, *The Clay Jar Review*, *Pure in Heart Stories*, and *The Way Back to Ourselves*. She is honored to have contributed to the Southern Arizona Press Anthologies. This is her sixth anthology.

She is also a published contributor to the books, *I Chose You, Rescue Dogs and their Humans* and *Chicken Soup for the Soul: Lessons Learned From My Dog*.

Her personal ministry is sending weekly cards of encouragement to those going through difficult times.

Poetry Inspired by "A Midsummer Night's Dream"

Magic

He:
It's magic that I feel for you,
For, lo, a spell you cast.
I couldn't dream of one like you,
And yet, your mine, at last.

She:
No, darling, it is I who feels
A spell is what you weave.
My words cannot express the depth.
Your love makes me believe.

He:
I'm overcome with love so strong;
I'd say, your love consumes me
Much like a fire that burns intense,
And still, somehow, it soothes me.

She:
Such love is one I've never felt,
Nor will I ever feel
For anyone but you, my love!
This love we share is real.

He:
I, too, feel so enchanted by
Your aura, form, your face.
I know full-well 'twill never change
By neither time nor space.

Solstice Triumph

In summers past when I was yours,
You were my heart's desire.
So loved was I, I can't deny
That kind of love, that fire…

Caused me to lose my way because
Your love, indeed, consumed me.
I didn't know what I would lose.
You had me so completely.

For I knew not that love like that
Prohibits any other,
No one to share my thoughts, my doubts,
Not even with my mother.

I thought that love like that would be
The answer I was seeking,
That it would bring me happiness.
But rather it was wreaking…

Such havoc with my loved ones who
Had always only sided
With me and what was best for me.
So mutually decided…

That somehow they would find a way
To rid me of love's focus.
They planned to dream a dream one night,
The night of summer solstice.

Poetry Inspired by "A Midsummer Night's Dream"

For that's the night, if one can dream,
That all one's dreams come true.
They thought it was the only way
To save me, bring me through.

That night as each one slumbered,
The dreams they dreamt came true.
The all-consuming love I had
Was gone and so were you.

The Fairy's Spell

The fairies dance amongst the flowers.
Those blossoms fragrant be,
Then I fall prey to such as this,
As fairies sing to me.

Intoxicated I must fall.
The fairies cast their spell.
No longer can my heart resist.
It leads to, who can tell?

It's strange that though I understand
What blindly I must do,
The fairies have me in their grasp,
Wish I could come to you.

Why is it so, I cannot tell,
But I am captivated.
They lead me to, I know not where
Their magic has me fated…

To follow where the fairies lead
I realize I must.
I follow blindly, I am lost.
Somehow their way I trust.

What is this place where fairies lead?
Succumb to this I know.
But when the journey ends then how
Will I know where to go?

Poetry Inspired by "A Midsummer Night's Dream"

Why do my queries fall upon
Deaf ears and leave me so
Bewildered, I may have to weep,
But wait…what is that glow?

It is the one who has beguiled
And lead me so astray.
It is the fairy by whose light
That I now find my way!

What was the purpose of it all?
I find it's so unclear.
Bewildered I. Must I now cry?
How have I gotten here?

But suddenly the focus comes,
My love, my heart, it's you!
I have been sent, not to lament,
At last, my searching's through.

You in my arms, awakened I
Will come to this conclusion,
Your love, it answers everything.
For you are no illusion!

My Dream

What can one say but dream we must,
Each night commands we do,
For in my dreams I see my love,
Not many nights but few.

But those nights that I dream of her,
My dreams, they fill me up,
And so at daybreak I'm fulfilled.
She brings to me a cup...

A cup of nectar from the flowers
That fills my very soul,
And all day long I think of this.
Within that thought I'm whole.

Though some would think that I must be
A fool to think like this,
I care not what those others think,
I'm dreaming of her kiss.

Someday I pray her love is mine.
In dreams I know 'twill be.
And so entwined forever then
Our love the world will see.

Poetry Inspired by "A Midsummer Night's Dream"

Scene from "A Midsummer Night's Dream" - 1873
John Simmons

 **Dennis Mitra Castillo** is a Filipino licensed teacher with 14 years of experience in teaching tertiary and senior high school levels. He holds a Master of Arts in Education major in Physical Education and a Bachelor's degree in Secondary Education with a major in Physical Education, Health, and Music and a minor in Social Studies. He is currently working at Malvar Senior High School. His passion in writing poems started during his college days where some of his works were published by *The Laser* - the official publication of Batangas State University – JPLPC Malvar Campus.

Poetry Inspired by "A Midsummer Night's Dream"

Enchanted Woodlands

Of the woodland fair where Shakespeare explored,
A place of magic, where the prompts bellowed,
With every stride, his stories were seeded,
His phrases were kept in the older trees.

The forest deep, where spirits swayed,
And fairies glided in a merry skipped,
With mischief and glee, they oft enriched,
The tales of fate and love, in a great affair.

In the heart of the woods, the stage was place
Where lovers met, and foes did perplexed
Amidst the trees, they played and conceded
Their lives unfold, with each new sketch.

Thus, let us explore into the woodland glow
Where Shakespeare's tales come to life in ray
Of the fairy valley and magical place
Where love was supreme, and magic thrives.

Lunar Mysticism

Under the calm radiance of the moon,
The world acquires a mysterious sheen,
as the wonders of nature become apparent and apparent.

The waves of the ocean are dancing with ethereal light.
And in a gleaming robe purge the globe,
as creatures emerge from their latent habitat.

Under the delicate and gentle moonlight,
The world is relaxed and moves more slowly.
As a sense of calm and peace spreads.

Poetry Inspired by "A Midsummer Night's Dream"

Love and Magic

In the middle of the woods, fairies roam,
On a midsummer's night full of joy,
Love and magic rule them all.

Four lovers lost, in the hypnotic haze,
Mistaken identities, a confusing maze,
But love prevails in this enchanted phase.

As dawn breaks, the spell vanished,
The lovers arise, problems resolved,
A cheerful ending, as the tale is told.

 **Jerri Hardesty** lives in the woods of Alabama with husband, Kirk, who is also a poet. They run the nonprofit poetry organization, New Dawn Unlimited, Inc. (NewDawnUnlimited.com). Jerri has had over 500 poems published and has won more than 2000 awards and titles in both written and spoken word poetry.

Night Music

I watch the fire dancing in the night
Illuminating swaying leaves of trees
In flickering and ever shifting light,
Both flame and foliage waltzing with the breeze.
And smoke invites the nostrils to inhale
The atmosphere, the scent of burning wood;
The moon, behind her gauzelike cloudy veil,
Looks down upon the scene and calls it good.
The crickets sing a song inviting all
To join in with the throbbing forest noise,
To answer the eternal wild call
Of nature and her elemental joys.
An evening of my favorite music by
An orchestra of earth, wind, fire, and sky.

Moonshine

The crescent moon hung languid in the night
Just dripping beams of liquid glowing light,
Anointing tops of trees and cliffs below
In silver drape of waterfalling flow,
Igniting lakes with luminescent shine,
And causing shadow vines to intertwine.
Reflecting off the rocks, it amplifies,
'Til moonlight spreads like swarms of fireflies,
It enters every corner, dark and deep,
And dances on our eyelids as we sleep,
And sprinkles dots of glitter through our dreams,
Reminding us that life's more than it seems.
The lunar radiance in shades of blue
Bathes jagged city streets in peaceful hue,
Makes beautiful the concrete jungle walls,
All slick and played with shade like marble halls.
That ghostly orb that daily rolls about
Makes all the Earth look different when she's out.

Poetry Inspired by "A Midsummer Night's Dream"

Summer Song

Summer bursts upon the scene,
Things with chlorophyl turn green,

Flowers bloom and bright birds sing,
Butterflies are on the wing,
Beautifying everything.
Growing grasses start to lean,
Busy bumblebees are seen
Tasting all the colored heads
Growing in the flower beds,
Yellows, purples, pinks, and reds.
Tuber, seed, and pod, and bean,
Vine and bud and in between,
Thriving, reaching, stretching out,
Doing what life's all about;
Count upon it with no doubt,

Summer bursts upon the scene,
Things with chlorophyl turn green.

Leanne Webber is a mother of two children and three cats. Much of her work is inspired by her interest in esoterica, feminism, and her background in psychology and trauma intervention. She currently works as a senior children's health advocate and a rape crisis worker.

Leanne started writing poetry at seven and won a few school-based competitions, including the school Eisteddfod chair competition for her poem about "The Future." She loves writing in general, but found she had little time for creative writing as she became more involved with her work and studies. She started writing again at 36 and has well over 50 pieces now published, both in print and online, and she has several poetry collections, in the pipeline.

Leanne feels that her soul is on a journey back to finding her authentic voice. She has also been dabbling with spoken poetry, now having performed live around twelve times, both online and at various local venues and events.

You can check out her spoken word videos on YouTube as "The Mystical Poetess:"

https://youtube.com/@themysticalpoetess5214

You can also find her on Instagram as @purple-persephone_ and on Facebook at Leanne Webber Poetry.

Leanne identifies as neurodivergent and as a solitary eclectic witch.

Poetry Inspired by "A Midsummer Night's Dream"

A Litha Blessing
(Shakespearean Sonnet)

The days are balmy, now Litha's here,
Sweet honey is offered by busy bees.
It's time for the longest day of the year,
As pollen's released from grasses and trees.

The summer Solstice has arrived,
The true apex of the sun hath come.
The flowers and the crops have thrived,
As solar storms seed visceral thrum.

The midpoint of the seasons' rise,
The horned god at his luminous peak.
The earth womb swells in soft reprise,
As Gaia unveils her yin mystique.

Light the bonfires in reverence and let's invoke -
The fae king and queen of the Midsummer oak!

My Mid-Summer Night's Dream

As the Solstice looms,
and lilac and honeysuckle blooms,
you are a dream that flows between
my sleep and wakefulness.
My eyelids try to grasp you,
before the fingers of my mind become too slick,
and you slink away, back to the netherworld.

As the weeping willows sway in the wind,
their pendulant branches stroking the mirror of my mind,
you are a trance that enchants the well of my desire.
My knees become feeble,
as a flash of your quintessence burns
a hole in my hippocampus,
and time melts into my skin.

As hot as a fever dream, the memory
of our own Bacchanalia ignites my shame
yet tickles the sweet spot of my inward senses.
You excite me as you elope further
and deeper into the forests of my slumber.
As I am lulled into the arms of Morpheus,
the more I want to fall into your versatile hands.
The harder I fall, the more potent
and magical the juice of the flower.

Poetry Inspired by "A Midsummer Night's Dream"

As pixies and dragonflies gather at summertime,
you mesmerise me with the steely cobalt of your eyes,
and it turns my thoughts blue as salvia.
Is this a spell or "love-in-idleness"?
Or simply the fruit of my own nature, at play?
I am as bewitched by you as Lysander was of Helena,
whilst the wisps of your arrow pierce my heart
and slide into my hypnagogic realm.

As the impishness of sprites and the wedding rites
of Theseus and Hippolyta echo in my consciousness,
the sting of love and lust gone wrong
wakes me from my drowse.
I wanted you as my perfect circle,
but the poison of reality formed triangles
and made our rousing bond futile
as the dark moon that birthed this reverie.

As fuchsias blossom and we stand
still in the sun, brief and elusive is the night.
We fancy what could be if the faeries
quit their meddling, and we are tantalised
by the promise of first rites.
When the membrane of the dream stays intact,
there is the escape of infinite reprise ...

But, if the limerence bursts
and the longing is consummated,
the fantasy might drift off ...
like a balmy summer breeze.

Free?

I planted my insides with a lush garden,
surrounded by a tall fence,
and dreamt that we looked over the edge,
to see the flying fish.
We gasped with awe and childlike wonder,
until I looked beyond,
and there asunder,
I saw the dark stagnant pool,
filled with the blackest beasts.
I felt like a fool,
as the elusive, mystical raven
and it's rare magic,
was seized, suddenly,
assumed ravaged,
by the savage, stealthy
swimming panther.

Then the old, wise man, the ancient sage
walked past from right to left,
gazed at me with knowing blue eyes,
left me bereft, with loaded words:
"it's wild out there."

The images blurred upon waking; the voice still heard,
resonating, reverberating through my bones.
The pool had no reflection,
but with time it all made sense.
Now sublime, condensed.
No longer wondering which creature outside the fence,
was the starring feature,
or which one was you and which was me.
Predisposed to play their primal roles.
Yet both within us and the two of them:

Free

Poetry Inspired by "A Midsummer Night's Dream"

Midsummer Night's Dream
Tales from Shakespeare – 1831

**Diane Sahms** is author of six poetry collections, most recently *City of Shadow & Light* (Philadelphia), Alien Buddha Press, 2022. She ios published in *North American Review*, *Sequestrum Journal of Literature & Arts*, *Brushfire Literature & Arts Journal*, *The Northern Virginia Review*, *POEMS-FOR-ALL*, *The Philadelphia Inquirer*, and *The Pennsylvania Literary Journal*, among others, with poems forthcoming from *Valley Voices & Home Planet News*. She holds a B.S. from East Stroudsburg University, with graduate courses and a secondary education teaching certification English from Holy Family University. She has taught high school English. She teleworks full-time for the government and is poetry editor at North of Oxford.

http://www.dianesahms-guarnieri.com/
https://dianesahmsguarnieri.wordpress.com/about/

Poetry Inspired by "A Midsummer Night's Dream"

Cock-A-Hoop Night

Once he, a Catbird,
and she, Holly's red berry
(cherry in the vulgar sense),

as if her purest fruit, temptation,
burned erotic, fiery power

a red, hidden sun buried within
young and unsophisticated.

Coy and shiverless, it was
an unflinching lure.

And beneath
a protective layer of skin,

optimistic naiveté
during frigid, blizzardly days.

No surprise then when he, as Catbird
hungrily eyed, she as in Holly's bush

through and throughout,
quickly plucked Holly's

ruby red berry
his catbird-bill breaking

the under skin
free from sight

on what should have been
a cock-a-hoop night.

 **Binod Dawadi** is from Purano Naikap 13, Kathmandu, Nepal. He has completed his master's degree from Tribhuvan University in English and enjoys reading and writing in literary forms, creating many poems and stories. His hobbies include reading, writing, singing, watching movies, traveling, and gardening as well as spending time with his pets. He is a creative person who does not spend his time by doing nothing; always helping those less fortunate. He believes that through writing and art it is possible to change the knowledge and perspectives of the people towards anything. He loves his country Nepal and has experienced the many cultures of his country as well as those of foreign countries.

His stories and poems have appeared in many anthologies and he has published his own poetry books: *The Power Of Words, Love and Life's Difficulties,* and *Nature, Animals and Human Beings* in Prodigy Published.

A Midsummer Night's Dream

I dream of doing a wedding,
But I have not found,
Any life partner up to now,
It is funny to listen,
I have danced and enjoyed,

In other people's wedding,
But I have no wedding,
It is better to do wedding with robots,
They are easily found in,
The market with the money,

They will obey all my orders,
Than the girl,
They have no emotions,
So, I can only be angry or happier to them,
I will enjoy my life with them.

 **Dibyasree Nandy** began writing in 2020 after completing M.Sc and M.Tech. She has authored poetry and short-story collections as well as full-length fiction. Her book of 200 sonnets is scheduled to be published in 2023. Many of her individual pieces have appeared in 58 anthologies and magazines. Her first work has been enlisted in the *Journal of Commonwealth Literature*. She is from West Bengal, India.

The White Night and the Black Sun

I paint a name in every heart;
You are but infants, unable to read; so start;
Blind I am, yet I enjoy throwing many a dart;
Once struck, they rotate; the gears of time;
It may not always begin with a floral gift, but a conflict or a crime.
Black Sun: You, an abomination, despicable;
Wishing to do away with the cold Moon, your sister sweet, evenfall's pinnacle;
Defeat you shall taste;
The lunar orb shall be freed from her shackle, her silver mien of snow replaced.
White Night: The shady dawn, meant to be ever bright, you are but a threat;
You raise your onyx blade merely for a debt?
What do you owe her? A battle with me just to return her to the sky?
A failure to erase me; do not try.
Black Sun: My partner in the heavens, a friend, contradicting existences we were;
All must be in equilibrium, I must make you concur;
Thankful I am, so I lift my sword against the end of the day which can never be aflame with light;
That is my obligation, that is what my soul decrees to be right.
I do not comprehend you;
What is your motive? What is your view?
White Night: A futile attempt;
For you trample on what is deemed sacred;
Never shall you know my reasons, even if I elucidated.
A fanged scratch in the alabaster eve;
A rip through the arrogance; the sterling eyes could not believe.
The dazzling sleeves of the lune seen;
Through the chains and past the jail bars, a smile, grateful, shimmers; a pearly sheen.

Black Sun: I would bring you down, I said;
It was no falsehood; you shall learn dread.
White Night: A glorious display, I commend;
However, if that is your extent…
A funerary column of threaded stars, a thousand celestial swords
    swirling;
From every direction they can strike, a brutal slaughter; the
    eternal eclipse ending;
But the grand hours late,
He uses but one starry blade;
Impaling;
The ebony Sol's scarlet rays spilling.
A frenzied panic;
"If I do not win, she will forever remain obscured; balance in the
    world no more;" a scream Satanic.
The veiled blazing beams lash out;
Inky yells screeching and loud.
Black Sun: Halt! Losing composure, never an option!
No enemy have I; this duel; one of opposing postulation;
Crimson tints not needed;
Stale concepts uprooted, left unseeded.
Come, my friend, I welcome, arms outstretched;
My lapse; temporary; no longer etched.
White Night: I see; noble you are; fair;
One final encounter, clean; would you care?
I shall divulge my thoughts then;
You, still fogged, still in sorrow, unable to bring joy to the world,
    misted by the grey rain.
Thus, feast your eyes on this pale steel;
Once it clashes with your dagger resolute, I desire to know what
    you feel.
Black Sun: A beautiful sight of finality;
But my iron weapon is too shadowed, extinguished, one of
    frugality;
Yet I shall endeavour to outdo;
To witness your spirit's hue.

A last confrontation;
One porcelain knife shatters, absolute triumph's creation.
White Night: O Victor, great opponent of mine;
Your obsidian brilliance and adamant might of charcoal diamond,
    I should have taken that as a sign;
Take off your cloak, I want to revel in your golden form;
You who entered my orbit like a comet bold, the whipping sun-
    storm.
Black Sun: Reveal the reasons;
For removing your sibling dear, she who controls the tides of
    seasons.
White Night: You talk of equality of contrasts, fool;
Yet you forget who I am; an alternate, someone who enforces a
    rule;
Neither of us should prevail;
Birthed we were to pen down polarity, not the Empyrean
    symmetry's tale.
In the azure, the Moon cannot be at par with your sphere;
No fellowship must bloom there;
I, the White Night, ready to restore the universe's natural order;
Even if it means my sister's oblivion and murder.
The mantle of insignificance you wore;
Befriending my family, you swore;
A fundamental cosmic flaw;
Yet you made me bow as you fought not me, but the law.
Black Sun: My comrade dear, why did you not say?
I could have kept your pain at my ignorance at bay;
Yes, this fight over the Moon's being shall cease and I, the Black
    Sun, will revert;
But she'll continue to beautify the Earth with her loveliness,
    wintry garb and shirt.
White Night: O Beloved, my tinge will darken too…
Black Sun: Please remain as you are, I love your appearance, that
    is true;
Live on, you are a beacon, persist as my guide;
Should I succumb to folly, my cherished hope in the gloom who
    grasps my hand as I hesitantly glide.

Southern Arizona Press

Richard Oyama's work has appeared in *Premonitions: The Kaya Anthology of New Asian North American Poetry*, *The Nuyorasian Anthology*, *Breaking Silence*, *Dissident Song*, *A Gift of Tongues*, *About Place*, *Konch*, *Pirene's Fountain*, *Buddhist Poetry Review*, and other journals. He has a M.A. in English: Creative Writing from San Francisco State University.

Bottom's Bottom Dollar

Who could love an ass's head?
The older I am, the more
Hangdog my countenance.
I'm transported to a nightwood.

A puckish boy drops a potion on
My eyes. I'm transposed to
Another key. The Bottom is the hollow.
Poor folk reside there, drinkin' home brew.

Monstrous, strange. I'm haunted
By the fierce vexation of a dream.

My artificer wakes me, making
Straight the conventions. It's
All airy nothing. I
Begin to discern shapes.

16/12/2020

Waiting for Kodak Express to digitize my memory
I sip iced lemon tea at Vanilla Cafe on an afternoon.
Dusty shadows of scaffolding fall across glass
Opposite the totalitarian hotel and bamboo walls,
Light from the atrium. I do not think of

Petticoats, patriarchy or patience nor
The lotus in the waterbowl but
Lorca's *verde, verde I want you.* I
Want that—an hour when
No funeral parades through my brain.

I thank Brigitte Bardot for
Reminding me I am alive.
Temple bells ring the demons
To hell.

Poetry Inspired by "A Midsummer Night's Dream"

My Mistress with a Monster is in Love – 1905
Charles A Buchel

Ann Iverson is a writer and artist. She is the author of several poetry collections including *Come Now to the Window*, Laurel Poetry Collective, *Definite Space*, and *Art Lessons*, Holy Cow! Press; *Mouth of Summer* and *No Feeling* is Final, Kelsay Books. She is also the author of a collection of creative non-fiction, *hen Eat My Love,* Southern Arizona Press. She is a graduate of both the MALS and the MFA programs at Hamline University. Her poems have appeared in a wide variety of journals and venues including six features in the Writer's Almanac. Her poem "Plenitude" was set to a choral arrangement by composer Kurt Knecht. She is also the author and illustrator of two children's books. As a visual artist, she enjoys the integrated relationship between the visual and the written image. Her artwork has been featured in several art exhibits as well as in a permanent installation at the University of Minnesota Children's Hospital. Currently, she is working on a book of ekphrastic poems and several children's picture book projects.

Poetry Inspired by "A Midsummer Night's Dream"

Moon Shadow

Once in a Blue Moon
the heart reconsiders
what she has considered
in all her considerations.

Reads again
the Book of Love
folds back the corner
of the most important page.

Twice in a Blue Moon
the heart makes no waves
on the silent sea of sky.

Early Morning, Crescent Moon

Weary
from her night shift
she reclines
into the starless sky
settles into slumber
like a sleepy sac of light.

What she dreams of
no one knows.
Into her darkness
only she goes.

Poetry Inspired by "A Midsummer Night's Dream"

Hermia and the Fairies - 1861
John Simmons

 **Andrew McDowell** became interested in writing at age 11, and by the time he was 13, he knew he wanted to be a writer. He is the author of the epic fantasy novel *Mystical Greenwood*. He has also written and published short stories, poetry, and creative nonfiction. Andrew studied at St. Mary's College and the University of Maryland, College Park. He is a member of the Maryland Writers' Association. He was diagnosed with Asperger syndrome, an autism spectrum disorder, when he was 14. Visit andrewmcdowellauthor.com to learn more about him and his writing.

Poetry Inspired by "A Midsummer Night's Dream"

Nighttime Crickets

Filling up the calm moonlit sky,
In chorus of an endless song,
They are passing these hours by.
Go out and listen to their chant,
As it either annoys the ear,
Or to the heart may this enchant.

Those nights clear in the dark thickets,
We know always of the crickets.

Creatures so small, sighted rarely,
Yet beyond a doubt they are there,
Coming in small numbers, barely!
Owls may hoot from time to time,
As might the screeching of the bat,
Yet they outlast all with their chime.

Those nights clear in the dark thickets,
we know always of the crickets.

#

Rhiannon Owens moved to Merthyr Tydfil from the North-West of England after bagging herself a handsome Welsh boy, Nicholas. She loves her cat, her mid-life crisis dresses, reading, and making her messy garden look even worse. As well as working on solo writing projects Rhiannon has had seven poetry books published along with her writing partner, the super talented Ashley O'Keefe.

Poetry Inspired by "A Midsummer Night's Dream"

Midsummer Night

Proud Titania, what visions has she seen?
This woman of strength and presence
This powerful Fairy Queen,

A quarrel over a changeling boy
Jealous Oberon, sought to bring her low,
To rock Bottom!

In the dappled light of a Midsummer's Eve
A farcical, fawning love
A slapstick tableau amongst the trees,

An evening as quiet as the days are long
A wife made subservient
Crooning her fool's lover song,

When her spouse and his minion
Grow tired of her shame
Dazed Titania comes back to herself,

...and she proclaims...

"What visions have I seen!
Methought I was enamour'd of an ass"

Proud Titania, such things came to pass
That man you love - that misogynistic, jealous ass...

Oberon is his name!

Dr. Genalyn Panganiban-Lualhati is an associate professor for the undergraduate teacher education programs at Batangas State University, The National Engineering University, JPLPC-Malvar, handling Teaching Internship, The Teacher and the School Curriculum, The Child and Adolescent Learners and the Learning Principles and Special Topics in Education. Apart from her teaching duties, she was designated as the College Focal Person for Internationalization in Action and Faculty Chosen by the University President as member of the Faculty Selection Board of the campus.

She is also a research-based faculty member who is trained in quantitative research, and with approved research for funding in the same university. Her research interests include environmental education, pedagogy and educational management, inclusive education and gender sensitivity. She has served as an internal examiner for student research and has published research articles in Scopus Indexed Journals, CHED accredited journal, ASEAN Citation Indexed journals, and in other international peer-reviewed journals with sterling reputation. She has presented research papers in national and international research fora. Moreover, she has published poems in an international book.

Her passion in teaching reflects her aim to mold education students to become academic leaders by instilling moral values and 21st century skills so that they can create for us a better future.

Poetry Inspired by "A Midsummer Night's Dream"

A Midsummer Night's Celebration

In fair Verona, where love did first bloom,
The stage was set for Shakespeare's comedy to loom,
With weddings aplenty and lovers' quarrels,
The woodland and fairyland, a world of morals.

Under the light of the moon, the fairies did play,
Puck's mischief causing chaos in his own way,
But in the end, love prevailed,
And the couples, happy endings, regaled.

The enchanted woodland, a place of wonder,
Where lovers did hide, their secrets to ponder,
And in the realm of fairyland, a magical place,
The fairies danced, with smiles on their face.

In this tale, love is the star,
Be it Romeo and Juliet, or Helena and Demetrius afar,
The plot lines interweave with grace,
In this play that leaves us in a happy place.

And so, we celebrate the joy and mirth,
Of Shakespeare's comedy, a treasure on earth,
With weddings, the woodland, and fairyland too,
Under the light of the moon, a story so true.

Enchantment Under the Moonlight

The woodlands echo with the sounds of mirth,
As Shakespeare's comedy takes birth,
With weddings and lovers' quarrels galore,
The realm of fairyland, a place to adore.

Under the light of the moon so bright,
Puck's mischief causes chaos and delight,
But in the end, love conquers all,
And the couples' joy, forever enthrall.

The woodland, a place of enchantment,
Where love is hidden, like a secret,
And in fairyland, a magical sphere,
Where fairies dance and laugh, without a care.

In this tale, love is the star,
The plotlines weaving near and far,
And we celebrate the joy and mirth,
Of Shakespeare's comedy, a treasure on earth.

Poetry Inspired by "A Midsummer Night's Dream"

Midsummer Eve – 1908
Edward Robert Hughes

 **Ken Gosse** usually writes short, rhymed verse using whimsy, and humor in traditional meters. First published in *First Literary Review–East* in November 2016, since then in *The Offbeat*, *Pure Slush*, *Parody*, *Home Planet News Online*, *Sparks of Calliope*, and others. He was raised in the Chicago, Illinois suburbs. Now retired, he and his wife have lived in Mesa, Arizona for over twenty years.

Poetry Inspired by "A Midsummer Night's Dream"

Perchance to Dream

There once was a midsummer's knight
whose dreams mingled love, hope, and fright
with an ass and a Puck
(neither hailed from Nantuck')
scored by Mendelssohn, to our delight.

 **Loralyn Sandoval De Luna** is a guest lecturer at the College of Teacher Education in Batangas State University-The National Engineering University JPLPC Malvar, Philippines. She finished her Doctor of Philosophy in Educational Management degree in 2019 while teaching in Thailand and has edited and written for creative publications under Muang Thong Thani Adventist International Church. She also previously headed the Publications Committee of Bangkok Advent School, Thailand. Aside from being an educator, she plays the piano and the cello with her musician friends in church. She also enjoys watering garden plants, watching television dramas, and reading.

Poetry Inspired by "A Midsummer Night's Dream"

Struggles of a Bewitched Human

The stars have lost
My thoughtless thoughts
A life, a love
Ways parted.
The moonlight dims
No grace within
A love, a life
conflicted.
Your smile reclaimed
My heart is saved
The love in life
Returneth.
For in your hands
Entwined with mine
This life with love
Rewarded.

**Gavin Prinsloo** is a resident of Cape Town, South Africa. He has been writing poetry since 2020 and has penned over 3500 poems to date. He has published his works in a series of three poetry books (*Pieces of My Mind Volumes 1 - 3*) with a fourth volume to be released in 2023 and two additional volumes scheduled to be released in 2023/2024. His work has appeared in Raven Cage and Dark Poetry Society Poetry and Prose Ezines and anthologies to include *Spotlight* (Jimmy Broccoli), *From Sunset to Sunrise* (Dark Poetry Society), *Dreamscapes* (Open Skies Collections/Shrouded Eye Press), and will be feature in *Impspired Volume 9*. All of his books and mentioned anthologies are available on Amazon.

He also creates video promotions and reviews on books, as well graphic poetry readings on TikTok and YouTube, under the profile Soul Whisperer.

https://www.tiktok.com/@tiktoktok_35?_t=8Uxd0HaBCEf&_r=1

https://youtu.be/RJcKm_ryzXw

Poetry Inspired by "A Midsummer Night's Dream"

Midsummer Morning

Lay thy hand in mine,
let thy will be mine to love,
Upon this morn of love divine,
glowing brightly from above

Puk has lain to rest,
his flute has its magic cast,
Asleep within a Midsummers Nights Dream,
His magic not meant to last

We stand beneath a blazing dawn,
where no man be still awake,
For dies be cast by flowers dew,
a misguided magic to his mistake

Lay aside the quarrels fought,
pray love with an open heart,
For even Puk and Faeries fate,
could not true lovers part

Lysander lays claim to Hermias Dream,
I surrender a peace to thee,
I am thy Oberon in Truth,
thou art Titania, lovers for eternity

Midsummer's Eve

I spied a dappled Puk,
among the sleeping gods he fiddled
Dancing to a pipers tune,
in his persistent voice he riddled

"What lies in wait but hath the temperament of gods indignant,
Who are treacherous in their endeavours, vicious and malignant?"

His cloven hooves struck a tapping on the ground, s
parks flew from steel shoe on rock entranced,
Around the sleeping forms he capered,
he fiddled and he danced
The breeze ruffled up his fur,
the moonlight glinted off his recurved horn,
A manic smile split his visage,
from him all madness born

"Death, fools, the answer is Death!" screamed he,
as he raised his flute to his lips,
As he played his malignant pipe,
sparks flew from his fingertips
His eyes they shone a deadly glow,
and in a corner a figure appeared,
As soon as he materialised,
Puk bowed as if afeared.

That night Puk took revenge,
the gods dispatched by the hand of Puks malicious mind
Death removed from the world of dreams,
no more gods on earth to find
So, on a midsummers eve,
listen for the song and sound,
Of music and gleeful laughter;
although the gods are gone,
their mischief is still around

Poetry Inspired by "A Midsummer Night's Dream"

Titania – 1866
John Simmons

Kay Lesley Reeves is a retired teacher, a UK ex-pat living in Spain with her husband and cat. She started writing poetry and short stories during Covid and has had work published in several anthologies.

Poetry Inspired by "A Midsummer Night's Dream"

Ariel's Plea

Pity me my agony.
A Sprite and Being of the air,
Rooted to the ground.
Bound and constricted,
Wounded by piercing thorns
By Sycorax, the evil witch.
Imprisoned in twisted trunk
Of yon enchanted tree.

Free me, oh great Prospero.
I will your servant be.
Your eyes and ears
If you will let me
I, Ariel, will be your slave.
At your command, the world
Will be, no barrier to me.

I'll work my magic in a night
But you are sworn
To give me back my flight.

**Joseph A. Farina** is a retired lawyer in Sarnia, Ontario, Canada. Drawing from his profession and his Sicilian-Canadian background, he is an internationally award-winning poet. Several of his poems have been published in *Quills Canadian Poetry Magazine, The Wild Word, The Chamber Magazine, Lothlorian Poetry Journal, Ascent, Subterranean Blue,* and in *The Tower Poetry Magazine, Inscribed, The Windsor Review, Boxcar Poetry Revue,* and appear in many anthologies including: *Sweet Lemons: Writings with a Sicilian Accent, Canadian Italians at Table, Witness from Serengeti Press,* and *Tamaracks: Canadian Poetry for the 21st Century.* He has had poems published in the U.S. magazines *Mobius, Pyramid Arts, Arabesques, Fiele-Festa, Philedelphia Poets.* He has had two books of poetry published, *The Cancer Chronicles* and *The Ghosts of Water Street.*

He has had poetry published in four previous Southern Arizona Press anthologies.

Poetry Inspired by "A Midsummer Night's Dream"

long night moon

cold moon
in your fullness
rising in gemini
silvered, celestial
lighting the darkness
of this season of man
as our roles in daylight ends
and your act in the heavens begins
outshining our coloured lights
and manufactured fairylands
in God's own fire
a beacon and promise
of the light's return

summer solstice

on the summer solstice
I dream of late nights full of light

Harleys thundering down desert roads
ridden by t- shirted adventurers
with biker babes in leather chaps
racing the late sunset

444's on interstates rumbling
their motors screaming freedom
tires smoking on hot asphalt
radios playing righteous brothers

young lovers walking river paths
speaking nothing their silence poetry

cold drinks on moonlit decks
reminiscing patio lanterns
hung on backyard porches
and my first kiss

Poetry Inspired by "A Midsummer Night's Dream"

Puck and Fairies
Joseph Noel Paton

 **Ken Allan Dronsfield** is a disabled veteran and prize-winning poet from New Hampshire, now residing in Oklahoma. He has seven poetry collections to date; *The Cellaring, A Taint of Pity, Zephyr's Whisper, The Cellaring, Second Edition, Sonnets and Scribbles, Inamorata at Twilight* and his just released book, *Aequilateralis, Aphorisms of the Water-Bourne.* Ken's been nominated four times for the Pushcart Prize and seven times for Best of the Net. He was First Prize Winner for the 2018 *and* 2019, Realistic Poetry International Nature Poetry Contests. He has begun producing Creative Content on his YouTube channel and has had success sharing his poetry with the social media community. Ken loves writing, thunderstorms, music, and spending time with his rescue cats Willa, Yumpy, and Melly.

Poetry Inspired by "A Midsummer Night's Dream"

Songs of the Garden Chime

Steal away during the full moon rising
the starlight kisses upon weary eyes,
relaxing, feeling the spirit drifting
and caressing the warming spring breezes.
Gentle songs whispered from the garden chimes
playing of sweet sonnets on a Sprites harp
softly releasing a crimson arrow
hits directly into my wanton heart.
Oceans of grass gently swaying in fields
near the granite stonewalls the Robin's bounce
enchanted orbs rise from bare tree branches
as squirrels and chippy's heartily chase
Your true love always keeps my heart smiling,
whilst the night stars flirt above garden chimes.

Soft Silky Breeze

Light winds move colorful leaves.
Branches sway in a slow harmony
roots spread in an opus of moonlight.
Frosted leaves lie lifeless in heaps;
victims of the autumnal dearth.
We commune with fairies upon a branch;
never argue with them while the moon is high.
Twinkling stars hide in shadowed clouds while
we sing a hymn to the winter queen;
A butterfly kiss finds my warm cheek.
It's hot and savory, like passion on lovers lane.
Her breath seems real and tastes sweet in darkness.
The rising bright full moon, like a slice of fresh lemon.
An epiphany creates uneasiness within the heart.
Self-righteous deviants answer only to the bullet.
Peace returns to a warm, bewildered forest in the Ukraine.
I sit quietly, with my rifle, in a soft silky summer breeze.

Poetry Inspired by "A Midsummer Night's Dream"

A Midsummer Night's Dream – Act 4, Scene 1 – 1857
Sir Edwin Henry Landseer

 **Matt McGee** writes in the Los Angeles area. His work has appeared in previous Southern Arizona Press anthologies: *The Poppy: A Symbol of Remembrance* and *Love Letters in Poetic Verse*. When not typing, he drives around in rented cars and plays goalie in local hockey leagues.

A Midsummer's Nightcap

Hannah and I had been binge-watching old M*A*S*H episodes and were on Season Six, the 'Comrades in Arms' two-part episode where Hawkeye and Hot Lips get stranded for the night in a little hut, when she said: "This is just like that time the four of us ran off for that weekend camping up in Piru." And I wondered if finally she knew, after all these years, what really happened the night we had gone off to the lakeside campground above Highway 126, on the edge of a California desert so close you can feel its hot breath blowing down upon your skin.

She and Eddie had finished a bottle of Don Julio, then passed out. Eddie's fiancée Amanda and I looked across the campfire and, bored, snuck away and hopped a ride with the park ranger into town. Across from a faded old building that had once been Dave's Feed & Grain glowed a little pub called Shorty's; we got a snootful, stumbled out the backdoor to an alley, wondering how we were going to get back now that the ranger had gone to bed for the night.

I was staring at an old advertisement painted on Dave's old brick wall, its paint faded for over forty years, when Amanda leaned in. Her lips came to mine, her warm hand slid along my chest, then pulled back as if she'd shook awake from a dream. I leaned back and said "I guess we're all feeling a few last minute jitters." She nodded, and we started to walk back to the campgrounds, guided by moonlight. "I wonder if I should get thyself to a nunnery," she smiled. I shook my head and, as our gait fell into lockstep, said: "I think that'd not only disappoint Eddie but be a perfectly good waste of a very good kisser." She smiled and we held hands the next mile, our own little pact, the one we still keep between just me, her, and the stare of a horse's watching eye. At first, I thought I'd dreamt him, but he turned out to be an old faded ad upon the wall.

I thought of him again this afternoon, when Hannah and I hiked out to the old M*A*S*H site in the Santa Monica Mountains. It's all still there, though the helicopter pad has crumbled down, the motor pool long-since driven away. The rocky hillsides remain, though, like the continuing stare of a horse that should've been one more forgotten and faded part of a life's landscape, worn by the thick and unceasing march of time.

Poetry Inspired by "A Midsummer Night's Dream"

Photo from the set of M*A*S*H
Matt McGee

Erin Jamieson holds an MFA in Creative Writing from Miami University. Her writing has been published in over eighty literary magazines, including a Pushcart Prize nomination. She is the author of a poetry collection (*Clothesline*, 2023) and four poetry chapbooks. Her latest poetry chapbook, *Fairytales,* was published by Bottle Cap Press.

She can be followed on:
Twitter: @erin_simmer
Facebook: erin.jamieson.52
Instagram: erinjamieson6

Poetry Inspired by "A Midsummer Night's Dream"

A June Retelling

The stars are endless
as moonlight floods
my lace train-
ethereal & cool
as I walk an aisle
of candlelight &
sweet white blossoms

She watches me
pixelated light
transforming a face
I've long known
despite empty chairs
where my family
should be

But it's imperfections
that keep me walking,
hair adorned with
a laurel made of branches
and wildflowers

How her suit is just
a bit too loose
my eyes smudged
from crying
how we nearly
forget our vows

This is not a dream
nor a tale
of star-crossed lovers

Just two women
committing to another
under moonlight

Poetry Inspired by "A Midsummer Night's Dream"

Hermia and Helena – 1818
Washington Allston

 **Irma Kurti** is an Albanian poet, writer, lyricist, journalist, and translator and has been writing since she was a child. She is a naturalized Italian and lives in Bergamo, Italy. All her books are dedicated to the memory of her beloved parents, Hasan Kurti and Sherife Mezini, who have supported and encouraged every step of her literary path.

Kurti has also won numerous literary prizes and awards in Italy and Italian Switzerland. She was awarded the Universum Donna International Prize IX Edition 2013 for Literature and received a lifetime nomination as an Ambassador of Peace by the University of Peace, Italian Switzerland.

Irma Kurti collaborates with various newspapers, magazines, and websites in Italian, Albanian, and English; she publishes interviews with various individuals in the international literary scene and translations of poetry from all over the world.

She is a member of the jury for several literary competitions in Italy. She is also a translator for the Ithaca Foundation in Spain.

Irma Kurti has published 26 books in Albanian, 21 in Italian, 15 in English, and two in French. She has also translated 15 books by different authors, and all of her own books into Italian and English.

Irma Kurti is one of the most translated and published Albanian poets. Her books have been published in the United States, Canada, France, Italy, Romania, Turkey, Kosovo, the Philippines, Cameroon, India, Chile, and Serbia.

She can be contacted at kurtial@yahoo.com

Poetry Inspired by "A Midsummer Night's Dream"

The Immense Summer Sky

I was waiting for a sweet word that night
that would've filled my soul with light
while above us just like a field of fireflies
expanded the infinite summer sky.

I was just waiting for a caress like a soft
wave of the sea two steps away from us,
but you simply spoke and I was surely lost
in a labyrinth of episodes from your past.

Your voice trembled and mingled with
the waves; in fragments it came to me as
all my illusions vanished. It was enough
just to live the magic of that moment.

My love prevailed in the atmosphere; it
was filled with scents, manifold sounds,
close and elusive. I felt so happy, drunk,
your words wrapped in light—a distant
lighthouse in a dark and remote harbor.

Days have passed, turning into months,
the skies have changed and become
leaden and gray. The clouds announce
the tempests, but I still have above me
that immense summer sky like a field—
boundless and unattainable—of fireflies.

Previously published in *One day you will tell me* (Southern Arizona Press. 2023).

 **Janet Ruth** is a New Mexico ornithologist. Her writing focuses on connections to the natural world. She has recent poems in *Tiny Seed Literary Journal*, *Fixed and Free Quarterly*, *Tulip Tree Review*, *The Ocotillo Review*, *Sin Fronteras*, *Ekphrastic Review*, and anthologies including *Where Flowers Bloom* (The Red Penguin Collection, 2022). Her sonnet "Invisible Before Us Untouched and Still Possible" won a Laureates' Choice Award in the 2022 Maria W. Faust Sonnet Contest. A series of five of her poems won the 2019 Tucson Festival of Books Literary Award for Poetry. Her first book, *Feathered Dreams: celebrating birds in poems, stories & images* (Mercury HeartLink, 2018) was a Finalist for the 2018 NM/AZ Book Awards.

https://redstartsandravens.com/janets-poetry/

Poetry Inspired by "A Midsummer Night's Dream"

The Door to Night is Ajar

Above my head an arc of ancient light
flows—a river through inky pre-dawn sky.
Across my view a flash of feathered night

twists and flutters wings in stuttered flight,
trails the banner of his dark, throaty cry.
Above my head an arc of ancient light

flares from long-dead stars, impossibly bright,
as silhouettes of shadowed absence fly
across my view. A flash of feathered night

sweeps the phosphorescent flames of starlight
from ghostly grasp of thorny branches high
above my head. An arc of ancient light

begins to pale—the dying of the night.
Milky river, with dawn's approach, runs dry.
Across my view a flash of feathered night

makes one last pass to hold in memory's sight.
Nightjar departs, bright'ning air breathes out a sigh.
Above, a fading arc of ancient light
and my last view, a flash of feathered night.

Originally published in *Sin Fronteras: Writers Without Borders*, Volume 24, 2020

A Midsummer Day's Dream

First spoke pierces ash-blue sky over Sandías,
second illuminates a macaw petroglyph on basalt
across the valley. Sparks fly where iron wheels
clash with rock at the Crest—the chariot
begins its roll up arc of New Mexico sky.
Embers add to growing heat, where they land
in tinder-dry duff—smoldering birth.

No need for bonfires to drive away dragons this day,
yet drought has left plenty of bleached bones for fuel.
No one need walk barefoot across glowing coals
to prove their faith—burning sand will suffice.

No nearby lake or ocean beside which to celebrate
the burning. The Río Grande twists and dribbles
at the whim of distant snowmelt, controls at Cochiti Dam,
acequia ditch-masters. She never escapes her banks.

Luminosity of waxing moon and diamond-studded night
fade behind Mount Taylor to the west. In the bosque,
stretched in dappled cottonwood shade, Titania recovers
from a night of revels with ass-eared Bottom,
while Puck winks in yellow-and-white robes, whistles,
flutters on olive wings. Having collected Gambel's oak leaves
on sere foothill slopes before dawn, a curandera threads her way
among shadows by the river, collecting yerba mansa
and other herbs—to weave into solstice wreaths,
to dry as medicines for a winter difficult to imagine
in this heat.

Poetry Inspired by "A Midsummer Night's Dream"

Chariot reaches the apogee of its arcing path—
time stands still for a moment. Charioteer flaunts
his blazing light. All of us swelter in the molten triumph.

Chariot horses with manes of flame scream,
impatient, stamp iron-clad hooves against sky,
then resume their journey, gallop down
the arc of heaven toward a string of sleeping volcanoes,
kick up clouds of dust and moisture
that build into blinding-white hoodoos.

Mortals below—
trapped between gods and dragons—
dream of rain.

 **Joan McNerney's** poetry has been included in numerous literary magazines such as *Seven Circle Press*, *Dinner with the Muse*, *Moonlight Dreamers of Yellow Haze*, *Blueline*, and *Halcyon Days*. Four Bright Hills Press Anthologies, several Poppy Road Review Journals, and numerous Kind of A Hurricane Press Publications have accepted her work. She has four Best of the Net nominations and her latest titles are *The Muse in Miniature*, *Love Poems for Michael*, and *At Work*, all available on Amazon.com

Poetry Inspired by "A Midsummer Night's Dream"

7 Summer Notes

Trees cascading over
emerald fields. Noon
swollen wet with green rain.

Listening as jingles
from ice cream vans
circle noisy streets.

Teenage girls parade
downtown showing off
their new sun dresses.

A red-hot rod passes by
streaming salsa music.

Children at Townsend Park
tumble down hillsides breathing
in fresh mowed grass.

Big hunks of strawberry pie
with gobs of whipped crème
at the picnic table.

Full moon anchored
between blue sky
and waves of clouds.

Summer Solstice

Trees outline the
horizon in green lace.
Beneath boughs float
galaxies of blue bugs.
Crimson clouds smudge
a sapphire sky.

Listen to swish of
branches as cicada
swell and swarm.
Hiding under shadows,
beating their wings,
hissing their mating calls.

Evening is coming…
the dawn of nighttime.
We are suspended now
between light and dark.
Clouds rushing over heaven.
Sun drops from sky.

The air is fragrant with
sweet blooming jasmine.
Southern winds sweep
across the hemisphere
brightening star after star
awakening this night.

Poetry Inspired by "A Midsummer Night's Dream"

The Birth of the Sun and the Triumph of Bacchus – 1761
Corrado Giaquinto

Karen A VandenBos was born, once upon a time, on a warm July morn in Kalamazoo, Michigan. She can be found unleashing her imagination in two online writing groups and her writing has been published in *Lothlorien Poetry Journal, Blue Heron Review, The Rye Whiskey Review, One Art: a journal of poetry, Anti-Heroin Chic, The Ekphrastic Review,* and others.

Poetry Inspired by "A Midsummer Night's Dream"

Night of the Long Sun

Summer solstice, night of the long setting sun, ruled by the Honey moon. A midsummer fire of oak and fir is stoked by the velvety taste of mead.

It is a night to leave cookies and cakes for the Faeries and beware of their mischief. An evening when the sun lasts long into the night and the forests are cloaked with love.

A night when frivolity rules and humans are led by the fiery heat of the late sun. A night when the forest is full of lust and hand fasting is done under a cathedral of trees.

It is the night when we dream of the secrets between the veils and the winds of time blow the wheel forward. The moon rises and fills with the scent of honey. The sun-drenched lovers clasp hands and dream of children.

 **Barbara Boothe Loyd** majored in Art History and English at the University of Maryland Ramstein Air Force Base campus in Germany where she graduated in 1974. By 1975 she moved to Houston, Texas, and enjoyed the stimulating art environment there. Fredericksburg, Texas, became the location for her studio in 1999 when she and her husband Paul and three pets moved to the Hill Country. In 2020, they settled in Granbury, Texas.

During her career, Barbara taught art to students from 1st-12th grades in public and private schools as well as adults. A perpetual student, Barbara obtained a teaching certificate from Sam Houston State University in Huntsville, Texas. Graduate level courses were added at Texas Tech University, the University of Texas at Dallas, and Rice University.

Barbara's memoirs have been published, as well as her poetry in numerous anthologies and magazines. In addition, she is an award-winning artist who has displayed her works in many local, regional, national, and international exhibitions.

Her social media link: Facebook as Barbara Boothe Loyd

Poetry Inspired by "A Midsummer Night's Dream"

A Midsummer Night's Mix-up

I am that merry wanderer of the night
Who chants faint hymns to the moon so bright
Over hill, over dale, over park ever pale.
I must seek some dewdrops here
And a pearl for each cowslip's ear.
In the night, imaging some fear
How easy is a bush supposed a deer.
Before night's swift dragons cut clouds full fast
And yonder shines Aurora's harbinger at last;
The iron tongue of midnight hath tolled twelve,
All lovers to bed, 'tis the time for elves.

 **Marieta Maglas** has poems published by *The Oddville Press, Sybaritic Press, Prolific Press, Silver Birch Press, Ardus Publications, Dashboard Horus*, and others as well as in anthologies like *Near Kin: A Collection of Words and Art Inspired by Octavia Estelle Butler, The Oddville Press Summer 2018, Nancy Drew Anthology: Writing & Art Featuring Everybody's Favorite Female Sleuth, Three Line Poetry, Tanka Journal, The Aquillrelle Wall of Poetry*, edited by Yossi Faybish, who also edited her poetry book, *Cubic Words*. She is a co-author for *A Divine Madness: An Anthology of Modern Love Poetry, Enchanted- Love Poems and Abstract Art*, and some other anthologies. She lives in France.

Poetry Inspired by "A Midsummer Night's Dream"

Pantoum for Summer

The rainbow's ribbons still stretching in the blue rain
Are like snakes waking up at the tune of the jazz flutes.
Butterflies chase bumble bees singing duets in vain.
Summer dances around some red roses and green fruits.

When the snakes wake up at the tune of the jazz flutes,
Summer slips over the meadow her dream of green.
She dances around some red roses and green fruits.
The moon rises from the cloud's fence like a queen.

Summer slips over the meadow like a dream of green
In a fall sky having puffy winds and a dim light.
The moon rises from the cloud's fence like a queen.
With green shadows, the sprites appear all around the sight.

The fall sky has puffs of clouds and a floating light.
Butterflies chase bumble bees singing duets in vain.
With green shadows, the sprites appear all around the sight.
Summer rainbow's ribbon still stretches in the blue rain.

 **Gitanjli Mridul** is a poet and teacher from India. She earned a Masters' degree in English Language and Literature. She is a hilly woman from the beautiful hills of the Himalayas and writes in her native language of Hindi as well as English. She is a nature-loving poet.

Poetry Inspired by "A Midsummer Night's Dream"

A Midsummer Night

A Midsummer night
An angel came in her dream
Waving wondrous wand
Luring with lascivious lute
Spell cast surreptitiously
Silently seducing the sheila

She fell for him !

Days and nights fly by
Murmuring whispering love sighs
Holding caressing sheen
Kisses and cuddles umpteen
Somber soporphic slumber
Entwined in embrace evergreen

Aah ! Evanescent dreams !

Rapturous reverie broke
Awoke the angelsome bloke
His soul's half remained in heaven
Had sold his soul already
Bound and tied in custody
He was only on parole

Oh! He had to go !

He rose to bid adieu
Tears were in her eyes
Suppressed were her sighs
Pale pearly penurious
She was an autumn tree
Forever thus she remains
A stunt on the barren land
Not ready to fall easily

She still hope to hear spring songs !

Poetry Inspired by "A Midsummer Night's Dream"

The Quarrel of Oberon and Titania – 1849
Sir Joseph Noel Paton

**Molly Howes** has been writing poems for some time but is a new submitter of poetry for publication. Her prose work has appeared in the *New York Times* "Modern Love" column, the *Boston Globe Magazine, Bellingham Review, Tampa Review,* and many other publications, as well as being listed as Notable in *Best American Essays*. She is a grateful recipient of fellowships to Ragdale, VCCA, A Room of Her Own, and MacDowell. Her nonfiction book, *A Good Apology: Four Steps to Make Things Right* (Grand Central Publishing, 2020) explores the meaning and power of making amends.

Her poems have appeared or are forthcoming in *The Mississippi Review* and *Offerings: A Spiritual Poetry Anthology from Tiferet Journal.*

After many years, she has become a New Englander, but she still returns to the Gulf of Mexico for long swims whenever she can.

Website: mollyhowes.com

Summer Magic

On this high summer day
in Maine
I've forgotten how to slow.
My long strides
pull me along the dusty road
as if against the clock.
Before me, amidst the gray and crunchy gravel
shadows begin to dance.
Prancing patterns of sunlight and shade
dapple the ground,
make it glimmer.

It's enough to stop my hurried tread
to make me search above instead
as a thousand leaves far overhead
wave their greetings down.
Do their tiny shifting shadows
cover me, too?
Do they dance across this damp
and hurried jogger?
Do I seem to shimmer too?

These leaves
backlit by a summer sky
are bits of magic –
they make me stop
and nod my own hello,
and remember again
to wonder.

 **Lucia Lemieux**, MFA retired from teaching English and Creative Writing at Newbury Park High School, Ventura County, California in June 2023. There she advised *Bold in Italics*, the literary magazine which she founded in 2014 and GSA for 12 years. Active in equity and LGBTQ+ issues, she received the Nancy Bailey Human Rights Award (2018) from the California Teachers Association, and in May of 2023 was awarded the WHO Award from CTA's Channel Island Service Center for her dedicated union work. She has been featured in several anthologies and has read her work widely—at the Taper, Beyond Baroque, before various legislative sessions and several venues throughout the nation (and Israel). Active in California Poets in the Schools from 1997-2009, she edited their 2008 anthology *On the Other Side of Tomorrow,* in which Al Young, then California Poet Laureate, wrote the foreword. She is a member of the Society of Children's Book Writers and Illustrators, and has contributed her work to ONTHEBUS, Spillway, Rattle, CWP, SCWRiP, Falling Star Magazine and others. She previously worked in Entertainment. Six full marathons, and countless other races earned her the nickname "Roadrunner." Originally from Michigan, California has been her home for 40 years.

Poetry Inspired by "A Midsummer Night's Dream"

An Early Spring Morning's Dream

To physically exist with both humans and fairies
Is second nature to me
Like breathing underwater
Or riding on the back of a lion.

I'm not sure whose company I prefer—
Both species can be dark and deceptive.
One is given magic, the other free will
Neither using either for good.

I'm the notable knight in the middle,
content to watch the highs and lows
struggling toward purple perfection,
to outshine the other, yet royally fail.

In winning, we may lose our goodness,
in losing, we may gain our grit.
Middling may give us nothing
except the status quo: complacency.

Yet, standing firm on middle ground,
where no one resides anymore
is what more of us need to do—
To hear the other and begin to understand.

Fae Folk in California

James M. Barrie wrote that
when the first baby laughed,
its laugh broke into a thousand pieces
and fairies were born.

I guess they must have reproduced,
and flew from Scotland to
California, because I have seen so many,
here in my home, escaping the cold.

I've seen Kelpies in Santa Monica—
They like to live by the water. Here, some of them
surf, but don't get near them. They feed on other
fairies and humans who get to close to their waves.

Brownies are common here, brought by immigrants.
they love the earth and if they like you
will help with chores around the house and garden.
Kind and benevolent, they don't like liars, cheaters—or cats.

Gruagach walks alone on the Venice Boardwalk.
She has a frightful face, but a golden heart.
Share your fire and she will bless you.
But she has ADD and sometimes forgets.

I saw Dryads once, in Sequoia National Park.
They are female but appear androgynous, like
Bowie in the 70s. They live in oaks and make music
humans cannot resist. If their trees die, they will too.

Poetry Inspired by "A Midsummer Night's Dream"

In my backyard I was buzzed by a hummingbird—
or so I thought. Turning slowly, I found a winged pixie
fluttering nearby. She took a drink from the feeder, sprinkled
dust and flew away. A rose bloomed there the next morning.

At Zuma in Malibu, past the huge waves, I swam.
A sun-filled day, I could see rays ten feet below me.
I was so mesmerized; I swam away from shore.
Merfolk offered me their hands, put me back on course.

These fairies wander our streets and beaches,
our forests and seas, sometimes looking like
everyday people trying to survive in an often-unkind world.
Whether they are barbarous or beneficent, depends wholly on us.

 **Mary Ann Cabuyao Abril** was born in Manila, Philippines in 1969, Dr. Mary Ann C. Abril has over 15 years of experience in teaching at the Batangas State University. Believer of Christ since 1986, Dr. Abril aspires to inspire through her creative works and give back the glory to Him in all her endeavors. A neophyte in writing poems, her works were published by the Southern Arizona Press and Culture Cult Press.

Poetry Inspired by "A Midsummer Night's Dream"

Gift of Litha

At the dawn of light on this wondrous day,
In the realm of enchantment where fairies play,
Mystical beings dance in a melodic tune,
As the arms of Litha finally unfold,
The gift of precious blossom, true miracle to behold,
A life, more valuable than gold.

Amidst the haze of patient-years,
Longing for the sweet laughter to echo in the breeze,
True love awaits, yearning in each passing day,
Till love essence emerges in the breeze of pure bliss,
The symphony of joy, so crystal clear,
A gift of love filling the days with great joy.

Your Hue

In the tranquil hours when daylight fades,
You emerge a silhouette in the fading light,
An ethereal beauty of mystic hue,
An enigma embraced in the cover of the night.

As the sky's canvas turns a gentle hue,
The sunset unfolds a magical sight of you,
A symphony of colors, a waltz of light,
Radiating love's essence, so gentle and true.

Your hue at twilight is a captivating sight,
Mysterious, yet inviting, igniting hearts to shine,
With warm caresses and tender embrace,
One finds love so radiant and divine.

Just as the sun surrenders to the night,
Let my heart basks in your majestic glow,
In twilight's embrace, let my love grow,
Be immersed in the allure of your hue forevermore.

Poetry Inspired by "A Midsummer Night's Dream"

The Awakening of the Fairy Queen Titania – 1790
Johann Heinrich Fussli

Mark A. Fisher is a writer, poet, and playwright living in Tehachapi, California. His poetry has appeared in: *Reliquiae*, *Silver Blade*, *Eccentric Orbits*, and many other places. He was nominated for a Pushcart Prize for his poem "papyrus" in 2016. His first chapbook, *drifter*, is available from Amazon. His poem "there are fossils" (originally published in *Silver Blade*) came in second in the 2020 Dwarf Stars Speculative Poetry Competition. His plays have appeared on California stages in Pine Mountain Club, Tehachapi, Bakersfield, and Hayward. He has also won cooking ribbons at the Kern County Fair.

Poetry Inspired by "A Midsummer Night's Dream"

Nick Bottom

"This is to make an ass of me," Nick said
as he fills his play with all his passion
coming straight out of his own donkey's head
and mixed it with a dose of compassion

that he gained for all lovers in his dreams
for no one knows how "these things came to pass"
and nobody is really who they seem
even to the one in the looking glass

but heart strings entwine and bind us despite
they cling merely to the shadows of love
that may fade if brought out into the light
and the seeing of our true selves thereof

dismissing mistaken identities
knowing real love with its complexities

Puck Laughs

In forest forsaken proud Titania
Clad in forest green damask finery
Plots reprisal as she sits upon a
Comely throne wrought of wood and ivory

As all the lovely fay prance before her
Seeking out her eye to be upon them
And to hear them speak in reverent verse
Distracting her seeing the world of men

And all the half-witted endeavors made
To entreat her into granting wishes
To the mortals that merely serenade
Her with their unbelieving kisses

All the while Oberon is still waiting
To shower him with her love unfading

Stephanie DuPont is a yoga instructor, gardener, designer, Etsy shop owner, artist, photographer, poet, and short story writer originally from Miami, Florida. She has also lived in Colorado and Leeds, England, but now resides in Atlanta, Georgia.

Stephanie has been creating stories for as long as she can remember. Her first was about a princess named Poppy and a horse named Fred. She enjoyed reenacting her stories with her brother Ryan – Stephanie played Poppy the princess and her brother Ryan played Fred the horse. The story and play were a huge hit in the DuPont household!

Stephanie has been acclaimed by the Jurica Suchy Museum's nature poetry competition. Her current work explores themes about history and the natural world. She especially loves conjuring short stories and poems about her native Miami.

You can also find Stephanie on:

Instagram: @glitterymoonvintage,
Twitter: @moonvintage.

A Dance Among the Chanterelles

Begin with stars. The woods are lit by dust
Of fairies frolicking in midnight dreams.
When fairies shine, they outshine even the moon;
They scatter dalliance of wanderlust.

Vanilla orchid vines perfume parades
Of rose and lilac's romantic embrace.
The songs are soaked in scents of silken blooms,
This night is sparkling. Chanterelles cascade

Under the shade of ancient wishing trees.
Prisms of pastel caps expand to conceal
A wolf who came to cause the wood's demise
By freeing poisoned spores into the breeze.

Within the woods, the legend of the wolf persists.
This scoundrel skulks in shadows, seething with hate.
With eyes ablaze with hunger's fiery mist.
Ignorance's bliss is death's kiss.

With a wheeze and a sneeze and a squeeze, the poison rains
On petals of narcissus and nightshade blooms.
Quixotic notes combine with anise spice.
The sultry stems and mushrooms drench refrains.

A willow weeps and seeps, as a dance ensues.
Turning points and trips on aesthete display,
When nubile nymphs arrive with the wolf's wife,
Oh my. A frightful sight. The wolf reveals his ruse.

The fairies gasp as the wolf's disguise is undone.
The wolf and fairies clash in a dizzying fight.
The wolf is captured, and condemned to confront
An endless curse: his wife. The wolf is shunned.

The dance is done. The crystal nightlight blends
Into a candy sky. The sleepy sprites
Ignite a spell to quell the woods from harm.
The forest drifts to sleep again. The end.

Regina Chriscel Santos Delute is an outstanding literature and language teacher with 12 years of expertise in the area She has spent the last eight years teaching at a college, where she has encouraged many students to fall in love with language and literature. She encourages students to think critically and imaginatively about the materials they study, and her teaching style is very engaging.

Ms. Delute is a researcher in addition to being a teacher. She has published two research related to her field, and both of them were received and published in an international journal. Additionally, Ms. Delute has presented her findings at academic conferences.

Ms. Delute is working on her dissertation on Philippine literature as she pursues her PhD in English. She is interested in critical racial studies, feminist theory, and cultural studies. Ms. Delute likes to read, write, and travel. In her free time, she creates engaging content for her students.

Poetry Inspired by "A Midsummer Night's Dream"

The Dance of Love

A midsummer night's dream
is all it really seems
in the stillest lake there was peace
a sauntering couple whispered and it was

for once they found merriment
in time alone with just the fireflies
within this predicament
there was just one thing that didn't sit right

the boy pixie does not know how to explain
how his heart flutters when his love looks back at him
he could only stare back at her face in the moonlight's glow
as she smiles back at him as she flies to and fro

she gently holds his hand
as they fly to the middle of the lake
enraptured in this magical dance
with that atmosphere she created

confused as the male pixie was
he could only comply
even though he was timid and shy
it had mattered not, for it was only them to see the sights

perhaps they were lovers
perhaps they were fools
but both were so fearful
of saying I love you

Paul Gilliland retired after over 30 years of service with the US Army and settled in the high desert of Southeast Arizona, just miles from the historic wild west towns of Tombstone and Bisbee. He holds Associate of Applied Science Degrees in Intelligence Studies, Linguistics, and Education from Cochise College; a Bachelor of Arts Degree in Music Theory/Composition and Technical Theater Design from Olivet College; and a Master of Fine Arts Degree in Music Composition from the Vermont College of Fine Arts. He is an educator, composer of 21st century chamber music, author, form poet, and publisher. He is a member of the American Society of Composers, Authors, and Publishers (ASCAP); National Writers Union; Authors Guild; Poetry Society of America; the Academy of American Poets; and the Association for Publishers for Special Sales. In addition to teaching interviewing techniques and report writing for the US Army, he is the Editor-in-Chief of his own publishing company, Southern Arizona Press. He currently has three published volumes of poetry, *Hindsights of 2020*, *The Journey of the Fool: A Poetic Journey in Three Parts*, and *A Heroic Crown and Other Sonnets*, all available through Amazon. He is currently working on completing his fourth collection of poetry, *Tales from a Southwest Inn*. His poetry appears online in numerous Facebook poetry group as well as being published in *Sonnet Sanctuary Anthology Volume 1* (A Romeo Nation), *Open Skies Quarterly Volumes 4, 5, 6, Perceptions, Dark Reflections*, and *Myths, Legends, and Lore* (Shrouded Eye Press), and *From Sunset to Sunrise* (Dark Poetry Society Anthology). When not busy with teaching, reading, editing, and publishing, he provides services as a Certified Expert Sound Healer.

He can be followed online at:

https://www.facebook.com/PaulGillilandPoetry
https://www.facebook.com/SouthernArizonaPress
http://www.PaulGillilandMusic.com/
https://www.SouthernArizonaPress.com/

Poetry Inspired by "A Midsummer Night's Dream"

Fireflies and Fairies

On warm summer nights
In June and July
When fireflies start
To light up the sky

The forests are filled
With sparkling light
From fireflies
That light up the night

The fairies emerge
With moondust in hand
To spread all their magic
Throughout Fairyland

The moondust, it mixes
With the fireflies glow

Fairies at Night

The woods are home to fairy folk
Who come out in the evening gloam
From dwellings in the mighty oak
Within the fields of sterile brome

They make their music all night long
While playing games and having fun
To each their favorite fairy song
They dance until the morning sun

Poetry Inspired by "A Midsummer Night's Dream"

The Shooting Star of Romance

A shooting star that flashes with bright light
Will give a spark of freshness to romance
So, make a wish before it's out of sight
A shooting star that flashes with bright light
The star that brings you fortune here tonight
Your love life through this omen will enhance
A shooting star that flashes with bright light
Will give a spark of freshness to romance

An Evening in Early June

The evening night is quiet and the trees, they softly sway
The balmy breeze a reprieve from the heat wave of the day
The sparrows and the finches with the titmice and the doves
Are nestled in their cozy nests in branches up above

The stars all twinkle brightly in the darkness of the night
While June's New Moon has risen but is hiding from our sight

From stars up in the heavens we perceive the slightest glow
Illuminating objects on the forest floor below
We sit now in the gloaming here beneath the swaying trees
And listen to the whispers of the balmy summer breeze

Poetry Inspired by "A Midsummer Night's Dream"

Summer Nights

I watch the stars come into view
With every evening night anew
While in the east the moon doth rise
And as the night gets ever dark
The stars across the sky embark
Upon their westward route reprise

Before my eyes, the bright moon glow
Enlightens all the world below
With luster shining through the trees
With pensive thought I lay below
The ever-changing nightly show
Accompanied by summer breeze

These times I seize without regret
Forgetting not the nights like these

Summer Solstice Sun

The midsummer solstice sun
Rising over the Sarsen Stones
Tells us summer has begun

Between the stones of grayish dun
Rising over sacred bones
The midsummer solstice sun

Litha starts its sacred run
And sounds of bagpipe drones
Tells us summer has begun

For as the morning dawn is done
The voice of a druid priest intones
The midsummer solstice sun

The tales of old that priests have spun
Explain the myths of great unknowns
Tells us summer has begun

The holiday of fire and fun
A prayer for each sin atones
The midsummer solstice sun
Tells us summer has begun

Poetry Inspired by "A Midsummer Night's Dream"

Previous anthologies from Southern Arizona Press

The Stars and Moon in the Evening Sky is a collection of 120 poetic works crafted by 65 poets from across the globe inspired by the universe around us.

Dragonflies and Fairies is a collection of 72 poetic works crafted by 34 poets from across the globe celebrating the magical and mystical creatures of folklore.

Ghostly Ghouls and Haunted Happenings is a collection of 129 poetic works crafted by 46 poets from across the globe inspired by ghosts, ghouls, and things that go bump in the night.

The Poppy: A Symbol of Remembrance examines the history of the poppy as a flower of remembrance, over 80 poems and lyrics written by World War One poets between 1912 and 1925, and 79 poems written by 21st Century poets from around the globe in remembrance of the fallen heroes from all war of the last century.

The Wonders of Winter is a collection of 120 poetic works crafted by 50 poets from across the globe that celebrate the winter season.

Love Letters in Poetic Verse is a collection of 143 poetic works written and contributed by 58 poets from across the globe celebrating romance and love.

Castles and Courtyards is a collection of 79 poetic works written and contributed by 37 poets from across the globe celebrating the medieval life of Kings, Queens, peasants, and troubadours.

Upcoming anthologies from Southern Arizona Press

Beyond the Sand and Sea – A gathering of poetic works inspired by the sea, seashore, lighthouses, or anything else associated with life on or near the sea. Coming in early August 2023.

The Children's Book of Bedtime Verse – A collection of poetic works appropriate for reading to children at bedtime. Coming in early October 2023.

Home for the Holidays – A holiday anthology of poetic works celebrating the gathering of family during the fall and winter holidays. Coming in early December 2023.

Poets interested in submitting works for upcoming anthologies are asked to check out our Current Submissions page at: http://www.southernarizonapress.com/current-submissions/ for more information about each anthology and our process for submission.

New independent releases from Southern Arizona Press

Poetry Inspired by "A Midsummer Night's Dream"

Lords of the Afterglow - Renegades and Noblemen by Judge Santiago Burdon is a collection of sixteen bizarre, precarious, as well as comical Bohemian tales of adventurous mayhem. While working as a drug smuggler for a Mexican Cartel, Santiago; a recovering addict, ex-con, womanizer, gambler, and ill-fated pilgrim encounters situations of irresistible misfortune. Adding chaos to these events is his ex-cellmate, loose cannon, drug and alcohol fueled Colombian partner Johnny Rico. It is an expedition into twisted and hilarious states of mind and body. Every story in this collection centers on the working relationship and unique friendship of these 'Dos Chiflados' Two Whacky Guys. *Lords Of the Afterglow* is a must read.

https://www.amazon.com/dp/1960038249

Freshly picked from the low hanging branches of my family tree ... What started off as a one-time introduction to describe where his thoughts had come from has become Ross Leishman's signature trademark. ***Lost Thinker - Unchained Melodies of Melancholy Harmonies*** is his first collection of 130 poems exploring life, love, and loss. This is a book that will have you savoring each page and reading over and over again. A wonderful bedside or travel companion.

https://www.amazon.com/dp/1960038230

Individuals interested in working with Southern Arizona Press to bring their books to print are asked to review our publishing services at:

https://www.southernarizonapress.com/publish-with-us/

Then Eat My Love by Ann Iverson is a small gem of an essay collection that portrays, with vivid granularity, the joys and sorrows of family, love and loss. Ann Iverson creates living, breathing characters who take life in these essays and will remain with the reader.

https://www.amazon.com/dp/196003815X

The Flight of a Dragonfly is a collection of Tanka and Cherita poems by Ram Chandran.

https://www.amazon.com/dp/1960038206

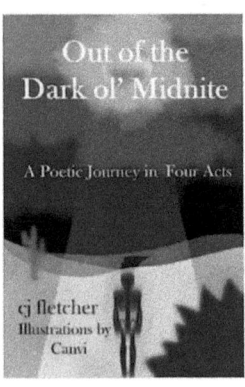

Out of the Dark ol' Midnite by cj fletcher is a composite of a lifetime of influences ranging from World Religions to Urban Legends. A World traveler, he's been a soldier, a counterintelligence agent, a security specialist, a singing cowboy, poet, songwriter, and guitarist. The songs contained in this book are real. They may be purchased at most digital music outlets. The albums are *ghost town* and *Ocean Boy*, both by cj fletcher. The music, poetry, and stories by cj fletcher are rife with clues, mysteries, and secrets. He invites you to unravel them. If you dare.

Poetry Inspired by "A Midsummer Night's Dream"

Southern Arizona Press

Published works by our featured contributors

Love Poems for Michael by Joan McNerney
Many reflect on New England with autumn foliage and fierce winters. However, four seasons do include bursting springs and boiling summers. Love is its own season, its own country, its own domain. Let's explore love up north during spring and summer.

https://www.amazon.com/Love-Poems-Michael-Joan-McNerney/dp/9388319656
https://www.cyberwit.net/publications/1602

At Work by Joan McNerney explores everyday workers. It is unique because each worker, either female or male, receives their own page. These are snapshots of people who are either content with or made unhappy by their daily circumstances. Reading this book is an exploration of human nature at its core.

https://www.amazon.com/At-Work-Joan-McNerney/dp/8182537835

https://www.cyberwit.net/publications/1759

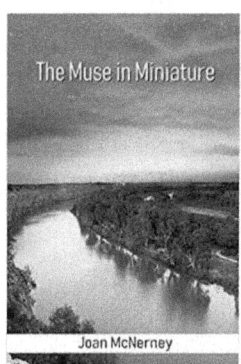

The Muse in Miniature by Joan McNerney
There is no doubt this poet very aptly traverses an immense range of emotion and experience. Here we find poetry's passion and powerful imagination in rich abundance.

https://www.amazon.com/Muse-Miniature-Joan-McNerney/dp/9389074509

https://www.cyberwit.net/publications/1262

Fireflies Beneath the Misty Moon is a collection of Ekphrastic poems written by Dibyasree Nandy inspired by the works of Japanese artists Okumura Masanobu, Suzuki Harunobu, Utagawa Kunisada, Yoshitoshi Tsukioka, Kobayashi Kiyochika, Ogata Gekko, Toshikata Mizuno, Settai Komura, Torii Kotondo, and Kondo Shiun.

https://www.amazon.com/dp/1960038125

One Day You Will Tell Me - Irma Kurti's book profoundly evokes the changes of time, its unstoppable evasion that makes us discover fragile, transient beings in constant evolution subjected to the inclement human weather of detachment, mourning, and absence. It presents a wide thematic variety, which makes it enjoyable and persuasive to the reader. We rediscover the feeling of nostalgia for the homeland but also get a look at the canonical existential vexations that situate humans in insurmountable aporias and impracticable dilemmas. Irma Kurti, who is a poetess inscribed in the etymological history of the word "poetry," shows herself to be an attentive and passionate woman when writing on paper, thanks to her brilliant attitude and the creative spark that propels her.

https://www.amazon.com/dp/1960038095

Poetry Inspired by "A Midsummer Night's Dream"

Aequilateralis - "Possessing a unique voice, Ken Allan Dronsfield has lured many a reader into his world of word play with his prolific writing on a wide range of subjects, but mainly his poetry relating to nature truly takes my breath away. He has the ability to reach a diverse audience; and he touches the heart and mind of all who enter the pages of his expressive and imagery-filled poetry books. After reading silently several times, I decide to read each poem out loud, words tumbling smoothly from my lips cascading down onto the previous, which then turn the experience into a theatrical realm with marked acts as if a play, enhancing this extremely entertaining book even more so than what the already brilliant command of his language usage had caught our attention with, in the first place." - Leslie De Luca, Canada

https://www.amazon.com/dp/1960038117

In ***Feathered Dreams***, Janet Ruth - ornithologist, poet, artist, and international birder - shares her love of birds through poem, story, and image. She relies beautifully on her scientist's eye and artist's heart to recreate the magic we can encounter when we stop to watch and listen. This collection of avian treasures is a "wingèd paean of gratitude for the wonders, the messengers that are birds." Feathered dreams drift on the wind of poems and memories in this love song to birds, to life.

https://www.amazon.com/Feathered-Dreams-celebrating-stories-images/dp/1940769957

An actor. A blue-collar worker with a haunted past. A casting agent and his receptionist. The characters of **Leaving Rayette** by Matt McGee move from one experience to the next, consuming, living comfortable and entertainingly rootless lives. Each of their stories overlap, and they eventually witness the effects on those they've left behind, and of being left behind by time.

https://www.amazon.com/Leaving-Rayette-Matt-McGee/dp/B0B7QG3FD6

In Diane Sahms's ambitious *City of Shadow & Light (Philadelphia)* there are classical elements, the prominence of the elegiac as well as the lyrical and an oracular power that echoes back to Greece, yet remains rooted in Philadelphia. The language soars—blooms, although with a dark undertone, illuminating the shadow and shading the light. Sahms's often heretical visions push brilliantly into an *unseen darkness*.

https://www.amazon.com/dp/B0BMSZ8NV8/ref=sr_1_2?qid=1668816380

Rhiannon Owens and Ashley O'Keefe join forces as Rhianno & Asley to take readers on voyages of poetic discoveries in the series of poetic collections:

A Voyage of Poetic Discoveries

https://www.amazon.com/Rhianno-Asley-Voyage-Discoveries-Collections/dp/B08B325GPT

Seeking Poetic Lands

https://www.amazon.com/Rhianno-Asley-Seeking-Poetic-Lands/dp/B08L7W5PWJ

Searching Across Poetic Sands

https://www.amazon.com/Rhianno-Asley-Searching-Across-Poetic/dp/B098GJDCTP

In Poetic Dreams

https://www.amazon.com/Rhianno-Asley-Poetic-Ashley-OKeefe/dp/B09SNW7G69

Nocturnals

https://www.amazon.com/Rhianno-Asley-Nocturnals-Ashley-OKeefe/dp/B0B5KQSKVN

Poetry is magic, weaving tapestries via lilting words, creating a stunning visual of the author's ideas. *The Power Of Words* is the debut poetry collection of author Binod Dawadi, edited by bestselling author Sydnie Beaupré.

https://www.amazon.com/dp/B0B3L6VLGG

Binod Dawadi's *The Life of a Vampire* follows Binod, who was not a bad vampire, he worked helping people and doing good things. The vampire kingpin heard of this and sicced evil vampires on him, forcing him to do terrible deeds. He refused because he is a true hero. Go on Binod's journey as he tries to find a woman as good as him, and as he tries to combat evil at every cost.

https://www.amazon.com/dp/B0B3GNQQFT

The Power of Words 2 is Binod Dawadi's sequel to the *The Power of Words*. A collection of poems and short stories about love, hate, happiness, sadness, wars, etc. to motivate people and make them aware of such things in life. The 26 letters of the alphabet are the twenty-six voices of God coming to earth to serve people in modern times.

https://www.amazon.com/Power-Words-2-Binod-Dawadi-ebook/dp/B0BB68KYW7

Gavin Prinsloo takes readers on a marvelous poetic journey of his work in a continuing series of poetic anthologies titles *Piece of my Mind*

A Mixed Genre Collection – Volume 1

https://www.amazon.com/Pieces-Mind-MIXED-GENRE-COLLECTION/dp/B095GNM3PX

Gods, Myths & Legends – Volume 2

https://www.amazon.com/Pieces-Mind-Gods-Myths-Legends/dp/B09ZD14972

Eros Awakened – Volume 3

https://www.amazon.com/Pieces-Mind-Gavin-Martin-Prinsloo/dp/B0B2TTVKNQ

Kevin's Nature Verses is Kevin Ahern's latest poem collection. In it, readers will find fun, funny, and insightful verses with a general theme of things about nature - the plants, animals, phenomena, and even nature in the greater universe. The book's over 110 pages of clever writing will leave readers chuckling and pondering simultaneously.

https://www.amazon.com/dp/B0C7JFHNW9

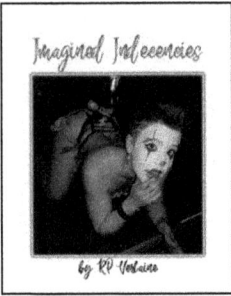

Imagined Indecencies is Rp Verlaine's third book. Poetry that is Profusely Illustrated with color photos taken by Verlaine of models and friends who posed for him. The poems are haiku, Seneru, sonnets, and one-line poems. A notable change from previous books is there are several free verse poems as well. All the poems have been published before in Literary Journals, Magazines, Newspapers, and websites. They have been published in Japan, Africa, Wales, Scotland and of course Verlaine's native America.

https://www.amazon.com/Imagined-Indecencies-Rp-Verlaine/dp/145663867X

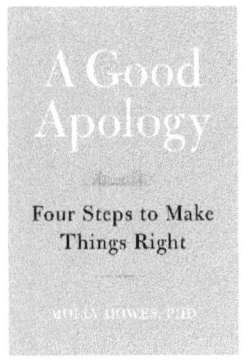

In *A Good Apology*, Dr. Molly Howes uses her experiences with patients in her practice, research findings, and news stories to illustrate the power and importance of a thorough apology. She teaches how we can all learn to craft an effective apology with four straightforward steps.

https://www.amazon.com/gp/product/1538701316